TOWARDS THE GOAL SUPREME
PARAMARTHA PRASANGA

TOWARDS THE GOAL SUPREME
SUPREME
PARAMARTHA PRASANGA

By
SWAMI VIRAJANANDA

Introduction by Gerald Heard
Foreword by Christopher Isherwood

Advaita Ashrama
Publication Department
5 Dehi Entally Road
Calcutta 700 014

Published by
Swami Mumukshananda
President, Advaita Ashrama
Mayavati, Champawat, Himalayas
from its Publication Department, Calcutta

ISBN 81-7505-032-2

Printed in India at
Trio Process
P-128 C.I.T. Road
Calcutta 700 014

Dedicated
With deep humility and devotion
To
SRI SRI SARADA DEVI
And
SWAMI VIVEKANANDA
In memory of
Their benign grace and benediction

PREFACE TO THE FIRST EDITION

For some time past revered Swami Vira-jananda, the present President of the Rama-krishna Math and Mission, had been putting down in writing, especially for the guidance of his numerous disciples, his thoughts and experiences on the subject of spiritual practice and discipline, as and when they arose in his mind. In order that they will be of great help to all seekers of Truth, whatever denomination they may belong to, the Swami, at the request of many devotees brought them out in book-form in the original Bengali. It was highly appreciated by the general public and the first edition was sold out in a few months necessitating a reprint. Pressed by his non-Bengalee disciples, he consented to translate it himself into English so that it may reach a wider public in India and abroad, and the present work is the result of his labours.

The Swami joined the Math (Monastery) then located at Baranagore, in the year 1892, after renouncing the world at the early age of seventeen. The long fifty-eight years of his life, since then, have been spent in intimate association and service of Swami Vivekananda and the other direct disciples of Sri Ramakrishna, and in scriptural studies and spiritual practices and austerities, and also in activities of various kinds while holding highly responsible positions in the Order. To him the world owes, not a little, for the compilation, editing and publication of the first five volumes of *The Complete Works of Swami Vivekananda* and the first edition of the four volumes of *The Life of Swami Vivekananda* by His Eastern and Western Disciples. A glimpse of the profound and varied experiences gained in all these years of strenuous spiritual endeavour and whole-souled devotion to the service of humanity comes to light in the present work.

It is not the aim of this treatise to discuss and solve big and abstruse metaphysical problems. The chief value of the counsels that follow lies in the practical hints, and in the inspiration they give to those who aspire after some sort of direct Realisation as a result of the awakening of the spiritual urge within, but who feel helpless and otherwise despair of success in their struggle against the various hindrances and obstacles, snares and pitfalls, currents and cross-currents, failures and disappointments of worldly life. It is hoped that the valuable instructions contained herein will help the disciple or the aspirant to advance with firm and reassuring steps along the road to the Highest Goal of life. A pertinent discussion and eminently practical solution of the various distracting doubts and problems, big and small, which daily confront the spiritual aspirant, mostly in the initial stage, is also a special feature of this book; yet it contains a large number of the high spiritual truths which form the basis of these counsels.

These instructions being given in an easy conversational style, are as refreshing and touching as direct talk, and being universal in their aspect can be easily understood and followed by all, men and women, learned and ignorant, young and old, householder and Sannyasin (monk), of all shades and creeds without distinction. The book is indeed indispensable to all

those who hunger and thirst after spiritual
life and for realisation of the Highest.

A glossary of Sanskrit words and Pau-
ranic names occurring in the book is
appended.

Mayavati   PUBLISHER
1st March 1949

INTRODUCTION

This book seems—to a Western reader —to be in the true tradition of Ramakrishna's and Brahmananda's teaching. Both in style and in spirit, in its practicalness and its topicality, it reminds us of M's great transcript of the Master's actual words, and of Brahmananda's teaching as given in THE ETERNAL COMPANION. In this book the reader will find no vague uplift or long sustained eloquence about generalities. The remarks show all the freshness of having sprung from actual talk and from the questions addressed to an authority by seekers of different competence and various proficiency. There is, then, something for everyone; and always there is that scientific exactitude, that sense of method and knowledge of technique, which is so often lacking in Western books on spirituality. Most people unacquainted with Vedanta, if they would pick up this book for the first time with an open mind, would find at least their curiosity whetted and perhaps their wonder aroused. If what is said here with such quietness—such assumption that it is true—*is* true—well then, surely everyone ought to do something about it. And it is that mood this book is meant to rouse. To those who have already made an effort to start upon the Way, it is full of useful information, sudden insights and profound counsels. Yet there is nothing in it that *is* startling or outré. It is clearly and surely in the Tradition—this is the voice of Ramakrishna, Vivekananda and Brahmananda; yes, and of the whole apostolic succession from the dawn of time, speaking today—speaking in the vernacular, speaking in those short paragraphs and pithy sentences which our hurried minds love, but speaking the Eternal Gospel, and of the lifelong—yes, many-lives-long—quest of the Soul for its one rest and reward.

GERALD HEARD*

* A well-known American writer and preacher.

FOREWORD

Here is a book written by a man of vast spiritual and, in the best sense of the word, worldly experience. As the President of the Ramakrishna Math and its widespread Mission, Swami Virajananda is qualified to speak both as a religious teacher and as an administrator of educational and social welfare projects. His words have therefore a double authority, and they are addressed not merely to monks but to all classes of men and women. Primarily, of course, the 'Paramartha Prasanga' is intended for a Hindu public, just as similar works written in the West are intended for readers whose religious background is Christian. But no serious-minded Western student should be deterred from studying it on this account. Even the noblest creeds and cults are only small provincial areas in the universal expanse of spiritual Truth. And, indeed, it may be positively helpful to a member of one sect to see this Truth stated in the terms and language of another. In this way, we may more easily distinguish between what is superficial and what is basic in our own beliefs.

Without attempting to summarise Swami Virajananda's message, I would like to mention briefly a few of its most important points—the most important, that is to say, to myself, for every individual will find here something especially relevant to his own problems and condition.

First, about spiritual disciplines, devotional acts, meditation and so forth. Don't argue about them; try them. 'I don't want to pray, but, by Jingo, if I do...!' is a very common attitude of intellectuals. The idea of the spiritual life attracts them philosophically and aesthetically, but somehow they can never quite decide how to set about living it. Before they begin, they must have their 'position' clearly defined, their 'case' precisely stated. They mistrust emotion, they must get everything straightened out in their rational minds, they say. And none of the existing religions satisfy them—some seem too old-fashioned, some too exotic, some dreadfully vulgar. Actually, they are mortally afraid of making fools of themselves, of being laughed at by their sceptical friends. So they talk and talk and read thousands of books, and time passes and they do nothing. This, as Swami Virajananda points out, is hopeless. Don't wait for a calm sea, he tells us. Plunge in, anyhow, anywhere, and never mind the waves. An ounce of spiritual practice is worth more than a ton of theology, and it is only through practice and first-hand experience that we achieve any degree of real wisdom. As this wisdom grows, the subtleties of dogma, which appear to the outsider as formidable obstacles to his faith, begin to seem very unimportant. That is why saintly men are sometimes found within even the narrowest and most intolerant religious sects.

Second, a word to self-doubters, backsliders and all those who are overburdened with worldly responsibilities and cares. Nobody is ever too busy, or too wicked, or too degraded to be able to pray. The man of affairs often dreams of the day when he will give up his duties and his business and devote himself to higher things. The drunkard plans to stop drinking and lead a disciplined life. 'The way I am now,' he says to himself, 'I'm not fit to approach

God.' These are dangerous and romantic notions. Even when they are put into practice, they are apt to produce exaggerated and hysterical acts of renunciation which can only end in relapse and redoubled self-disgust. We must start where we are, from what we are, and not overtax our strength. And we must not be ashamed of our lapses, as long as the will to struggle on persists. Sri Krishna said that no one who has once asked the way to God is ever lost—for, despite all appearances to the contrary, every step ever taken along that path remains a permanent advance. Acts of devotion and spiritual recollection, however slight and irregular, have a very strange power. Even when they are practised in seemingly flat contradiction to the mode of a man's life, they will slowly transform that life, though he may never make any conscious decision to live better.

This brings me to a third point—the last I shall mention here. In what manner are we to receive that first, small but decisive impulse which is to jog us out of our apathy and hesitation and start us on our way? This is a very individual question.

but I think this much can be said: Religious sentiment is seldom, if ever, aroused by intellectual argument alone, nearly always by example and some kind of personal contact. True spirituality is very infectious. A teacher's own life and faith speak much more loudly than his words. And that is why I recommend the 'Paramartha Prasanga'. It is something more than an ordinary book—it is a personal contact with a great man, a teacher who has actually experienced what he teaches. When we read in the newspapers about the political happenings in a foreign city, we are inclined to believe something of what we read, but a doubt remains; accurate reporting may be mixed with propaganda. When our best friend returns from that city and confirms the story, then we are very, very nearly convinced. But, to be absolutely and entirely certain, we must go to the city and see for ourselves. I hope that, for many readers, the ending of Swami Virajananda's book will mark the beginning of their own journey.

CHRISTOPHER ISHERWOOD*

* An American author and novelist of worldwide reputation.

2

but I think this much can be said. Religious
sentiment is seldom, if ever, aroused by
intellectual argument alone, nearly always
by example and some kind of personal contact. True spirituality is very infectious. A
teacher's own life and faith speak much
more loudly than his words. And that is
why I recommend the Paramhansa Ba-
sanga. It is something more than an ordinary book—it is a personal contact with
a great man, a teacher who has actually
experienced what he teaches. When we
read in the newspapers about the political
happenings in a foreign city, we are inclined
to believe something of what we read, but
a doubt remains; accurate reporting may
be mixed with propaganda. When our best
friend returns from that city and confirms
the story, then we are very, very nearly
convinced, but, to be absolutely and entirely certain, we must go to the city and see
for ourselves. I hope that for many readers, the reading of Swami Vivananda's
book will mark the beginning of their own
journey.

CHRISTOPHER ISHERWOOD.
An American author and novelist of worldwide
reputation.

श्रीरामकृष्ण-स्तोत्र-दशकम्

ब्रह्म-रूपमादि-मध्य-शेष-सर्व-भासकं,
भाव-षट्क-हीन-रूप-नित्य-सत्यमद्वयम् ।
वाङ्मनोऽति-गोचरञ्च नेति-नेति-भावितं,
तं नमामि देव-देव-रामकृष्णमीश्वरम् ॥१॥

आदितेय-भी-हरं सुरारि-दैत्य-नाशकं,
साधु-शिष्ट-कामदं मही-सुभार-हारकम् ।
स्वात्म-रूप-तत्त्वकं युगे युगे च दर्शितं,
तं नमामि देव-देव-रामकृष्णमीश्वरम् ॥२॥

सर्व-भूत-सर्ग-कर्म-सूत्र-बन्ध-कारणं,
ज्ञान-कर्म-पाप-पुण्य-तारतम्य-साधनम् ।
बुद्धि-वास-साक्षि-रूप-सर्व-कर्म-भासनं,
तं नमामि देव-देव-रामकृष्णमीश्वरम् ॥३॥

सर्व-जीव-पाप-नाश-कारणं भवेश्वरं,
स्वीकृतश्च गर्भ-वास-देह-पाशमीदृशम् ।
यापितं स्व-लीलया च येन दिव्य-जीवनं
तं नमामि देव-देव-रामकृष्णमीश्वरम् ॥४॥

तुल्य-लोष्ट्र-काञ्चनञ्च हेय-नेय-धी-गतं,
स्त्रीषु नित्य-मातृरूप-शक्ति-भाव-भावुकम् ।
ज्ञान-भक्ति-भुक्ति-मुक्ति-शुद्ध-बुद्धि-दायकं,
तं नमामि देव-देव-रामकृष्णमीश्वरम् ॥५॥

सर्व-धर्म-गम्य-मूल-सत्य-तत्त्व-देशकं,
सिद्ध-सर्व-सम्प्रदाय-साम्प्रदाय-वर्जितम् ।
सर्व-शास्त्र-मर्म-दर्शि-सर्वविन्निरक्षरं,
तं नमामि देव-देव-रामकृष्णमीश्वरम् ॥६॥

चारु-दर्श-कालिका-सुगीत-चारु-गायकं,
कीर्तनेषु मत्तवन्न नित्य भावविह्वलम् ।
सूपदेश-दायकं हि शोक-ताप वारकं,
तं नमामि देव-देव-रामकृष्णमीश्वरम् ॥७॥

पाद-पद्म-तत्त्व-बोध-शान्ति-सौख्य-दायकं,
सक्त-चित्त-भक्त-सूनु-नित्य-वित्त-वर्धकम् ।
दम्भि-दर्प-दारणन्तु निर्भयञ्जगद्गुरुं,
तं नमामि देव-देव-रामकृष्णमीश्वरम् ॥८॥

पञ्च-वर्ष-बाल-भाव-युक्त हंस-रूपिणं,
सर्व-लोक-रञ्जनं भवाब्धि-सङ्ग-भञ्जनम् ।

HYMN TO SRI RAMAKRISHNA

I

To Him, the God of gods, Bhagawan
                              Ramakrishna—
Who is verily the Parabrahman Himself,
In Whom inhere all cosmic birth and
                              growth and death
Who is untouched by the six *Vikâras*,
Whom words cannot express, nor minds
                              conceive—
                    The Eternal Truth Itself
Beside Whom no second exists,
To reach Whom sages follow the path
                              of Negation alone,
        —(" 'Not this, not this,' art
                              Thou, O Lord"),
            —I bow down in deep reverence!

II

To Him, the God of gods, Bhagawan
                              Ramakrishna—
Who dispels the fear of Devas, the sons
                              of 'Aditi',

Who destroys the demons, the foes
                of the gods
Who fulfils the desires of the good
                and the righteous
Who relieves the heavy weight of the
             sins of the world, and manifests
         His own true self in every age,
       —I bow down in deep reverence!

III

To Him, the God of gods, Bhagawan
                Ramakrishna—
Who has bound all beings in the
              cord of Karma,
Who brings all *Jnana* and *Karma*, all
          virtues and vices, each in its measure,
           into His own judgment,
Who dwells in our heart as intelligence
         and is the Witness unattached,
Yet from Whom emanate all actions
             that bind and free,
       —I bow down in deep reverence!

IV

To Him, the God of gods, Bhagawan
                Ramakrishna—

Who redeems all sins of individuals,
Who being the Lord of the Worlds
    was born out of compassion,
    of the womb of a mother
And accepted the bond of the body,
    of His own will,
Who lived the life beatific, displaying
    His sport divine,
  —I bow down in deep reverence!

V

To Him, the God of gods, Bhagawan
    Ramakrishna—
To Whom gold and potsherd were
    the same
Whose mind rose above all likes
    and dislikes
Who saw in all women 'Mahâ-Shakti',
  The Mother of the Universe Herself,
To Him, the giver of Knowledge and devo-
tion, of enjoyment here and hereafter,
of Salvation and pure intelligence,
  —I bow down in deep reverence!

VI

To Him, the God of gods, Bhagawan
    Ramakrishna—

Who inculcated the One Truth that is
　　　　　revealed in all faiths,
Who realised the truth in all creeds and
　　　　still had no creed of His own, no sect,
Who saw into the heart of all scriptures
　　　　　and yet was Himself unlettered—
　　　　　　　the Omniscient,
　　　　　—I bow down in deep reverence!

VII

To Him, the God of gods, Bhagawan
　　　　　　Ramakrishna—
Whose beauty made Him enchantingly
　　　　　　attractive to all,
Who often sang in rapturous notes
　　　　　songs to Mother Kali,
Who, in chanting grew mad in ecstasy and
　　　was wrapped ever in divine communion,
Who, by His sage counsel, guided the
　　　　　　aspirant's course,
Who dispelled the sorrows and heartache
　　　　　　　of all,
　　　　　—I bow down in deep reverence!

VIII

To Him, the God of gods, Bhagawan
　　　　　　Ramakrishna—

Who bore witness to the mystic virtue
                       of His 'Lotus Feet'
The dispenser of peace and happiness,
Who augments the welfare, here
                       and in worlds beyond,
                       of His own devoted children,
The scourge of the proud, the Fearless,
Who bodied Himself as the Teacher
                       of the World!
          —I bow down in deep reverence!

IX

To Him, the God of gods, Bhagawan
                       Ramakrishna—
Who was Paramahamsa's self on earth,
Withal, Whose nature was like that
                       of a child of five,
Who radiated happiness all round,
Who vanquishes all attachment for
                       the world,
In Whom dwell all Peace and Happiness,
Who demolishes the fear of birth and death,
          —I bow down in deep reverence!

X

To Him, the God of gods, Bhagawan
                       Ramakrishna—

Who checked the growth of unrighteous-
　　　　ness and redeemed *Dharma* from
　　　　　　　　　　all stain.
Who, though a Master-seer of truths
　　　　　　　　of all religions,
For guidance of men followed the
　　　　　　　　path of the 'many',
Whose holy 'Lotus Feet' should always be
　　　　worshipped by those who have
　　　renounced and those who have not,
　　　—I bow down in deep reverence!

XI

This ten-versed Hymn unfolds the
　　　　　　glory of Sri Ramakrishna,
Who was verily the God, Supreme,
　　　　　　　　Absolute, Himself.
He who reads this every day overcomes
　　　　　　　　　all dangers.
Japa and Tapa, Yajna, Yoga and Bhoga—
All such things may be easily attainable
　　　　　　　　sometime or other,
But a deep attachment for and devotion to
　　　Bhagwan Sri Ramakrishna is a rare
　　　　　　achievement indeed!

XII

Here ends Srimat Swami Virajananda's
exquisite Bhakti-promoting ten-versed
Hymn to Sri Ramakrishna, composed
in the 'Tunaka' metre.

———

TOWARDS THE GOAL SUPREME

PARAMARTHA PRASANGA

PARAMARTHA PRASANGA

—TOWARDS THE GOAL SUPREME—

1. To realise God an aspirant must have: Patience, Perseverance, Purity of body and mind, Intense desire or yearning, the aggregate of the Six Attributes, namely, Shama (tranquillity of mind), Dama (restraint of the senses), Uparati (giving up of attachment to objects), Titikshâ (remaining unaffected amidst all kinds of afflictions), Shraddhâ (faith in the words of the spiritual teacher and the scriptures), and Samâdhâna (concentration of mind on the Chosen Ideal, or God).

*　　　*　　　*

2. Do not tell anybody else, except the Guru, the realisations, the visions, or similar experiences, that spiritual practices may bring to you. Always keep your spiritual treasure—your inmost thoughts—hidden within you. These are not for vulgar gaze. These are your sacred possessions to be shared only between you and the Lord in secret. Likewise, do not talk of your defects and blemishes to others. You lose

3

thereby your self-respect and the respect of others for you. They are for you to confess to the Lord. Pray to Him for strength to overcome them.

* * *

3. When you begin meditation, first sit steadily for a while and watch the mind; let it wander wherever it pleases. Think that you are the witness, the seer. Sit watching how the mind floats and sinks, runs and skips. Keep thinking, "I am not the body, nor the senses, nor the mind; I am altogether separate from the mind. The mind, too, is material; it is only a finer form of matter. I am the *Atman* (Self), the master; the mind is my servant." Whenever any idle thought arises in the mind, try at once to put it down forcibly.

* * *

4. Ordinarily one breathes through the left nostril at the time of rest, through the right at the time of work, and through both at the time of meditation. The state most favourable to meditation is when the body and mind have become calm and there is even flow of breath through both

nostrils. But do not pay too much attention to watching your breath, nor make this a guide by which to regulate your activities.

*

5. When the mind is absolutely calm, breathing becomes steady and Kumbhaka (retention of breath) follows. When breathing is steady, the mind becomes one-pointed. Bhakti (love of God) also brings about Kumbhaka without effort and breathing becomes steady. Even without practising Yoga, Prânâyâma (control of breath) is attained automatically if one remembers and thinks of the Lord and does Japa with a yearning heart.

* * *

6. There is no other easy or convenient method to achieve one-pointedness of mind except by Abhyâsa, or repeated and sustained efforts, and by Vairâgya, or non-attachment to worldly objects.

* * *

7. Whatever be the time you devote to Japa and meditation—even if it be only ten or fifteen minutes—do it with all your

heart and soul. The Lord is the Indweller, the Inner Guide. He sees your heart; His measure is not how long you meditate on Him nor how many times you do Japa, but by your inner longing.

*   *   *

8. In the beginning, Japa and meditation taste rather dry. Yet you must go on practising them, even if it be like swallowing medicine. You will find joy after you have practised steadfastly for three or four years. Then, if you miss your meditation even for one day, you will feel miserable—out of joint, as it were.

*   *   *

9. Self-effort (Purushakâra) is necessary for spiritual attainment. Resolve firmly, "I will realise God through my own efforts by doing spiritual practices," and go on steadfastly practising Japa and meditation, seated in proper posture, for at least two hours every morning and evening, for three or four years—and see if you succeed or not.

*   *   *

10. It is not good for householders to do

much Prânâyâma or Yoga. Those who
are bent upon doing it, should strictly
observe regularity and moderation in all
walks of life. They should have nutri-
tious and Sâttvic (pure) food at the proper time, well-ordered activities, a life
without worry, a healthy and secluded spot
with pure air and temperate climate, clean
bowels, moderation in speech. Above all,
it is imperative to observe Brahmacharya,
or perfect continence. Violation of these
restrictions is liable to cause heart or brain
disease.

*   *   *

11. When by continued practice of Japa
and meditation, the mind will have become
calm and purified, then mind itself will be
your Guru, or guide, and you will have
proper understanding of everything, and
find the solutions of your spiritual doubts
and questions within yourself. The mind
will tell you what you should do, one thing
after another, and how you should conduct
yourself.

*   *   *

12. When doing Japa, meditate on the
form of your Chosen Ideal also; otherwise

Japa never becomes deep. Even if the whole
form of the Deity does not appear in
meditation, begin with whatever part of
the form comes. Try again and again, even
if you fail. Why should you give up, if you
do not succeed? You have got to carry on
with tenacity. Does meditation come easily
by the mere wish? Repeated efforts should
be made to collect the mind from other
objects and fix it upon the object of meditation. Success in this will come as one
goes on practising.

*   *   *

13. Japa, or mental repetition of the
Mantra, counting it on the fingers, using
a rosary, or keeping the number of the
repetitions—all these are only preliminary
means to help withdraw the mind from
other objects and fix it on the object of
worship. Otherwise, you will not know
when the mind may have run away in
another direction; or you may even have
dozed off. So, though these processes may
appear to some to cause a little distraction
at the outset, they will enable one to keep
watch over the mind's vagaries, detect
them easily, and draw the mind back and

keep it fixed on the object of meditation.

* * *

14. Never think yourself to be weak. Have firm faith in yourself. Think, "There is nothing that I cannot do; I can do everything if I will." Why should you acknowledge defeat to your mind? Know that if you can subdue it, the whole world will be under your feet. One who has no self-confidence does not have real faith in God. Swami Vivekananda has said that the real atheist is he who has no faith in himself. Nobody listens to the words of one who has no self-confidence; and God also does not listen to his prayers.

* * *

15. Asana is that posture in which one can sit for meditation steadily and with ease for a long time. But the spine has to be kept straight, and the chest, neck and head should be held erect, so that the entire weight of the upper part of the body may fall on the ribs and the chest may not sag. A stooping posture, in any case, is not healthy.

* * *

16. Your mind will inevitably be restless at the time of meditation so long as the idea has not taken firm root in you that the world is insubstantial and transitory, and that He alone is the only Reality. Love of God will grow and at the same time the mind will become calm to the extent that one is freed from the thirst for sense pleasures. All the pleasures of the world will become trivial and distasteful if even a particle of His Love is experienced.

*   *   *

17. Japa, meditation, ritualistic worship, prayer, remembrance, reading sacred books, association with holy men, godly conversation, retiring into solitude and thinking spiritual thoughts—whichever of these attracts you, according to mood and opportunity, and gives you joy, take advantage of that and do that. But meditation and Japa are the main things. Never miss them for a single day, however occupied you may be, or even in times of sickness or infirmity, in misfortune or calamity. In such circumstances, if you cannot or do not

find it convenient to carry on your practice in full measure, make salutation, pray and do Japa for at least ten or fifteen minutes.

* * *

18. The sensible man does not try to diagnose his own disease and prescribe medicine for himself by reading medical books. In case of disease, a doctor's advice should be sought. In the same way, if after reading many books and scriptures one proceeds to choose for himself a particular spiritual discipline, his mind may become confused and troubled by doubts and misgivings, progress may be interrupted, and waste of effort and even harm may result. The reason is, that the various scriptures contain divergent or even contradictory directions and methods, suited to aspirants of different temperaments and capacities, and different stages of life. It is, therefore, dangerous in many cases to decide for yourself what is exactly suitable for you. The Guru alone can direct you to the right path. That is why spiritual knowledge has to be acquired direct from the Guru. Know that the initiation and instructions given by him are the only path

for you to follow. If you do the spiritual practices as enjoined by him unswervingly and with full faith in them and in him, you are sure to achieve success in course of time. In any event, never give up these practices and take to other methods under anybody else's advice. If you jump from one thing to another, the only result will be that you will lose your way and drift about, without gaining anything.

*   *   *

19. Faith works wonders—makes the impossible possible. Faith plies its boat, setting sail over dry land. The doubting self is drowned even in ankle-deep water.

*   *   *

20. Hope is life. Hope is the source of all strength and effort. If hope is given up, one suffers agonies of death, becomes dead though living. Cling to hope till the last breath. Never, till death comes, give up the hope of realising God. If He so wills, He may shower His grace upon you at any time. Have this faith that He may perchance reveal Himself to you even at the last moment.

*   *   *

21. When God in His boundless mercy has, through the Guru, imparted the Siddha-mantra (mystic formula of the particular name of the Deity) which is the key to the portal of His sanctuary—know that He has given Himself away freely. But it is necessary for you to have that firm conviction. If you lose that invaluable jewel through carelessness and negligence, know that you are unfit for His grace. The right appreciation of this gift is the practice of the Mantra and the instructions imparted by the Guru with your whole heart and soul until the Goal is reached. Only by so doing will you be able to repay a part of the debt to him. The more you realise that God is nearer and dearer to you than your near and dear ones, the more you will be the recipient of His grace. Through His grace you will be free and ever blissful even in this life.

* * *

22. Until Love and Devotion to God grow, one cannot be aware of the transitory and insubstantial nature of the world. The mind is but one; and it cannot be partitioned into compartments, one part given

to God and other parts filled with desires for name, fame and sense objects. God cannot be realised unless the whole mind be given to Him. Unless one can do that, one has to be born again and again in the world and suffer endless misery.

*   *   *

23. In order to renounce the world, one need not take to holy orders or retire to the forest. Real renunciation is of the mind. If you give up the world mentally, it is the same whether you remain in the world or the forest. If you run away to the forest, without completely renouncing from your mind attachment for worldly objects, the world will follow you there also and trouble you just the same; there will be no escape from it.

*   *   *

24. If you have to be in the world at all, make God your world. Set up your home with Him. Whatever you do, see or hear, think that to be God. It is all play, a game with Him. Know life to be a game, in which Mother Herself is the Player and you are Her playmate. The

world will be quite different when you know that Mother is playing with you. Then you will find that in this world there is neither happiness nor misery, good nor evil, attachment nor aversion, greed nor jealousy. Consequently, all delusion, self-interest and conflict will vanish, and no pairs of opposites can torment you there. All ideas of union or separation, of friend or foe, of high and low, of 'I and mine', are non-existent in that play of yours with the Divine Mother. There is only—inexhaustible Bliss, boundless Love, and infinite Peace. If even a drop of that Bliss be experienced, the pleasures of worldly objects will seem contemptible. The possession of even an atom of that Love will make the whole world dearer than one's dearest ones, and heavenly Bliss will be felt through every pore of the body. There is no fear in that play, no anxiety, no bondage, no weariness; it is always an ever-new play. And what infinite modes of play does the Mother know! Endless are the forms and ways in which She plays! One loses oneself in the very thought of it and is merged therein. In that moment

of transcendental ecstasy the play ceases;
for who will then play, and with whom?
That beatific experience, that state of blissful union, is beyond the reach of speech
and mind! He alone knows who knows!
Great fun! Oh, the great fun!

* * *

25. We want to enjoy all the pleasures
of the world to the full and to have the
realisation of God at one and the same time.
Vain dream! It cannot be done, my friend.

* * *

26. If God comes and says: "What do
you want? Do you want me—or do you
want to live a happy life full of name,
fame, health and wealth for a hundred years
with wife, children and grand-children?"—
you will find that, except, perhaps, for one
in ten million, all will eagerly pray for the
latter.

* * *

27. To realise God one must devote
oneself to the task heart and soul—a
hundred per cent. Not even less by a
millionth part of one per cent, or the
minutest fraction thereof, will do. What

almost all of us seek is to realise Him easily, without much toil and trouble, and without sacrificing anything. We want to compromise between God and the world. We think that if the Guru out of his infinite mercy can get Him for us, and give us salvation, nothing could be better than that. Alas, how can this be? "The Lord must have His entire due, settled and squared to the last farthing."

*　　*　　*

28. He who really wants Him finds Him; he who does not, is made to dance to the tune of the five devils, becomes the sport of the five elements, which comprise the material of the body and the universe—earth, water, heart, air and space. He is at the mercy of evil influences of all kinds.

*　　*　　*

29. Swallowing an advertisement, many run after buying gold at half a rupee per *tolá*! But genuine gold alone is gold; something merely glittering like gold is not gold, but fake and spurious. You only lose the half-rupee!

*　　*　　*

30. Prayer does not consist in reciting

a set formula. That bears no fruit whatever. You must feel a real want within
for what you pray, suffer intense pain and
agony so long as your prayer is unfulfilled.
You have to be restless to find out the way
and the means of gaining the object of
your prayer, in spite of insuperable difficulties in your path, and to strive heart
and soul to achieve it, as if life itself
depended upon it. Only then will your
prayer be answered and your heart's desire
be fulfilled. Only such prayers reach the
throne of the Most High.

* * *

31. Highest knowledge, devotion, spirituality—these can only be acquired through
great self-effort. One has to struggle hard
to win them. Then only do they become
one's own, and enduring, filling the mind
with joy unspeakable. None can make a
gift of these to another. Spiritual practice
has to be diligently performed. Then only
can Realisation be attained. The degree
varies with the intensity of spiritual effort.
What is gained without discipline or hard
labour loses its gravity, is not highly
valued and does not bring happiness earned

by hard struggle. Moreover, it goes away as easily as it comes, and it is of little use when we are buffeted by the angry billows of life. In dangers and difficulties, in trials and tribulations, it is swept away altogether. To make spirituality one's very own, means saturating oneself thoroughly in the idea of the realisation of the Self, so that one's nature is wholly changed and an entirely new personality is developed. It is like being reborn again in this very body. Is it child's play? Such a thing is possible only if one is wide awake and strives for it to the utmost, as if one's whole life is at stake. Thus one must continue spiritual practices without interruption and with single-minded devotion as long as the Goal is not achieved.

* * *

32. If you give up your small self for the sake of others, you will not only find your real Self, but will also make others your own. The more you seek to save your little self, the more you lose your true Self and estrange others.

* * *

33. Go on struggling ceaselessly. Fight

like a hero. Never look back, but ever go forward. Onward to the Goal! Pay not the slightest heed whether you be exhausted, mangled or mutilated on the way. *Abhíh, Abhíh!* Be fearless! Courage! Courage! Do not allow even the thought of defeat to enter your mind. Realisation of the Goal, or let the body fall!—let this be your Mantra. Victory or death!—let this be the stake. If you have to die, die like a hero. Only thus can the fort be stormed.

* * *

34. Whining or self-pity is of no use at all. "I am too wretched, worthless, vile and weak; I cannot do anything by myself." These are the words of the namby-pamby, the do-nothing imbeciles. Can anything be done by such people? Strive hard, be wide awake and push on. Only then will success come. Will the road come to an end if you merely sit and think, "Oh! the road is long and difficult"? Get up, start walking, and as you proceed the road will grow shorter. Courage, strength, hope, unexpected help, will come. The path will gradually become

easy and straight, and, in no time, you will reach the goal. Oh! the joy of the fulfilment!

*   *   *

35. Many are under the impression that if they are initiated by an enlightened (Siddha) Guru, all their miseries will be dispelled in some mysterious way through his grace, if he only wills it! Thus, incurable diseases will be healed; employment after the heart will be secured; they will have worldly happiness and prosperity; will be able easily to arrange suitable marriages for their daughters; will have success in school or college examinations; will win law-suits, and prosper in trade and business; will get rid of their family troubles; will be able to escape the evil influences of an unlucky star like Saturn, and so on and so forth! There is no end of their supplications to the Guru! They ought to know that there is no connection whatever between initiation, or entering upon the spiritual path, and these trivial mundane matters. It is also childish to solicit such favours from the Guru; it is not at all a sign of spirituality. He is no

omnipotent Providence, no Dispenser of
earthly gifts, no Ruler over the destinies
of the people of the world. It is wrong to
embarrass or trouble him by such importu-
nate requests. They rather tend to make
the disciple an object of the Guru's dis-
pleasure than a recipient of his favours and
blessings. The relationship between Guru
and disciple is of a purely spiritual nature—
pertaining to spiritual matters only.

*   *   *

36. Service or worship with a desire for
the fruit thereof is mere shopkeeping.
True spirituality is not won with this outlook, and whatever result is obtained is
extremely meagre and evanescent. Worship
with desire for fruit does not purify the
mind. It gives neither supreme devotion
to God nor salvation, nor abiding peace
and joy. Sri Ramakrishna could not accept
or even touch things offered to him with
some underlying desire or motive.

*   *   *

37. To realise God in this life one has
to do Sâdhanâ (spiritual practices) with
all one's strength and ability, to offer one's
all to Him—and if possible, a little more.

As Sri Ramakrishna used to say, have faith and devotion, in even more than full measure. The meaning is, that one should become like a vessel overflowing with faith and devotion. How many have this abundant measure? There is, however, no cause for despair. Go on with your Sâdhanâ to the best of your ability. But always have this firm conviction that however hard you may strive, it is as nothing—it can never be enough—when the Goal is the realisation of the Self; for ultimately this Goal can only be attained by His grace.

* * *

38. But the grace of God descends only upon him who has striven his utmost, who has not spared himself, who has not let go the helm, and who has finally come to know, after many a hard struggle, that it is impossible to realise Him through self-effort alone—without His grace. When the aspirant feels that he is lost in impenetrable gloom, that he is about to drown in a boundless sea, his strength utterly exhausted by his efforts to keep afloat—then and only then does the Lord lift

him up with His lotus hand and take him beyond the realm of life and death, where there is endless bliss and infinite peace! The possession of even a particle of that bliss makes the Jiva or individual soul feel happy beyond measure.

*   *   *

39. Why should you fear the world so much, as if it is going to devour you? Be brave and fearless! Be a hero and make light of the world, and the world will lose its hold upon you. "I am very weak, I am low and sinful, I am worthless. Nothing can be accomplished by me, I am incapable of doing anything"—unless you give up such baneful ideas you will never succeed in achieving anything in life. Sweep those ideas away from the mind, stand up, and say like a hero, "What is there that I cannot do? I am the child of Immortality: Immortality is my birthright, nothing can dispossess me of that!"

*   *   *

40. Whenever weakness or listlessness assails the mind, recite the following verse:

"I am divine and nothing else.
I am Brahman the Absolute;
Misery and grief cannot touch me.
I am Existence-Knowledge-Bliss.
I am ever-free by nature.
O, my mind, say—Om! Tat Sat Om!"

*   *   *

41. Remember the Lord and think of Him as much as you can. Know Him alone as your own, nearer and dearer than your own self. He who is your sole refuge and resource, here and hereafter, love Him alone, with all your heart and soul. One thinks of the beloved and, thinking, gets joy and happiness thereby; one desires to be always in the company of the beloved, resents other topics of conversation or distractions that take one away. Nevertheless, such earthly love, like everything else in the world, has separation and end. But there is no end to the love of God. It is an inexhaustible treasure! The more you drink of it, the more thirsty you feel; and ultimately, losing yourself in bliss, you forget yourself and are merged in it. Then, this little individuality will melt away and divinity will take its place; in place of

this corpse-like existence, the divine consciousness (Shivahood) will illumine the soul; the dance of death will cease for ever and you will attain to Immortality.

* * *

42. You have read and heard enough of spiritual counsel. If you do not try to follow such counsel even to some extent, in your daily life, no amount of it will bear any fruit. Nobody will be able to get anything done for you; you will have to do it yourself. God will help you and bestow His grace upon you if you set yourself to work in dead earnest. Even God Himself carries the burden of such a one upon His shoulders and leads him part of the way. First, self-effort; next, Grace; finally, Realisation of the Reality.

* * *

43. It is extremely difficult to acquire true spirituality. All cannot have it. One must have some intrinsic substance within—past good deeds, or inborn impressions and tendencies for good, straightforwardness, sincerity, a feeling of inmost want. Even the Master (Sri Ramakrishna), who was so loving and full of

mercy, would not look at those whom he found to be "wet sapwood"—requiring too much blowing to light—in other words, thoroughly worldly-minded people. He used to say: "Realisation is not for them in this birth."

* * *

44. Practice of Japa and meditation unduly prolonged through sheer force, which brings on a feeling of extreme tiredness or exhaustion, should be avoided. It does more harm than good. Increase the time and energy devoted to Japa and meditation slowly and gradually. If there be sincerity, depth of feeling and firmness of purpose, you will have everything you desire in the fulness of time, through His grace.

* * *

45. Go on practising Japa and meditation with great devotion, perseverance and patience. Gradually the mind will become tranquil and meditation will deepen. You will feel a craving for your meditation, so that if you fail to do it any day, everything will taste insipid and you will feel out of joint and extremely uneasy, like an addict

missing his drug at the accustomed hour.
You will long to remain immersed in meditation, alone.

*　　*　　*

46. Brahman and Shakti, Purusha (Pure
Spirit) and Prakriti (Nature) are two in
one and one in two, and are in reality
non-different. The idea of separation lasts
only so long as we have the sense of duality
and the notion of the worshipper and the
Worshipped.

*　　*　　*

47. It is very good to dream of the Guru,
the Chosen Ideal and of gods and goddesses. It encourages and delights the
mind greatly. But do not feel unhappy
or dejected if you do not often have such
dreams. If you experience them, do not
go about talking about them to anybody
and everybody; you can tell them to your
Guru, if you like. Do not, however, rack
your brains to find out a meaning for
every part of the dream. A dream is
merely a dream after all, and it is idle to
expect integration and coherence right
through it. That happens only in the case
of *adesha*, or direct Divine Commission or

guidance, or of intuitive perception during absorption in meditation, or in Realisation —the truth of which leaves no room for doubt, and the possession of which transforms the whole life of a man and makes him divine. Such an experience does not come to anybody and everybody; it depends upon long and austere Sâdhanâ, or spiritual practices, and upon His grace.

* * *

48. Some receive a Mantra in dreams. But in many cases, such a Mantra is found to be not one as enjoined by the Shâstras, but one that is born of one's own imagination or leanings. If, however, one goes on steadfastly practising Japa of that Mantra with firm faith, Realisation may come from that also in course of time.

* * *

49. Practise your meditation in a lonely spot, in dim light or in darkness. Wear loose clothes and breathe through the nose keeping the mouth shut. Try to turn the senses inward at the time of meditation. Close your eyes and fix your mental gaze upon the heart, that is to say, deep within

yourself; and think that the Chosen Ideal
with shining form is residing there.

*   *   *

50. While you meditate, forget self-
identification with the body, that is to say,
give up the idea that *you* are this body.
Think yourself to be of the nature of the
subtle entity upon which the consciousness
of *aham*, or I-ness, that is, the idea of 'I
and mine', is superimposed; and think of
the Chosen Ideal as of the nature of unconditioned consciousness—ever-pure, ever-free
and self-luminous—bereft of all limiting
adjuncts. Think, while meditating, that He,
as Pure Consciousness, is pervading your
ego-consciousness; and your self—the ego-
consciousness—is within Him—the Pure Consciousness. In reality, you are of the same
essence as He, the difference is only in the
degree of manifestation. All this requires
spiritual practice for its true understanding
and cannot be conveyed in words. "Jiva
—the individual soul—is the Self in bondage,
and Shiva—the Pure Spirit—is the Self
without bondage."

*   *   *

51. While sitting for meditation, direct

the train of your thoughts as follows, and pray: "O Lord, from the ultimate stand-point I am of the same essence as Thee. This miserable plight of mine is the result of my being bound by Maya or illusion and deluded by a sense of 'me and mine'; of identifying myself with the body, and of my being a slave to evil thoughts, evil desires and evil tendencies. Thus, O Lord, I have become afflicted with sickness, sorrow, misery, wretchedness, fear and rest-lessness; have become mean, low and impure, and subject to death and to the tyranny of worldly objects; I am helpless, resource-less, destitute, small, weak and worthless. Be Thou kind to me, O Lord, out of Thy infinite mercy, and destroy all my sins, faults, wants and miseries, root and branch, so that I may awaken the infinite power which is lying dormant and lifeless within me; so that I may realise Thy Ever-True Nature; so that I may realise that which is my true nature—the eternal, ever-pure, ever-free, ever-luminous Self!"

* * *

52. To meditate on the Chosen Ideal, it is essential for one to have a little imagina-

tion, a little vision. It will not do to be
unimaginative, as dry as wood, and to hold
a too matter-of-fact materialistic attitude.
Thus, the form of the Ishta, with a benign
countenance, should be imagined and visual-
ised as residing in the cavity of the heart,
or in the lotus of the heart. Likewise, the
six mystical circles of the Yoga system—
the six lotuses, or nerve-plexuses—have no
material existence in the human body and
cannot be seen by the eye. They have to be
imagined and thought of by the initiated,
as sources of great power lying dormant
within. They have to be awakened by Yoga
practices. The more profound and deep the
meditation, the more pure and concentrated
will the mind become, and the more will
that power, dormant within, wake up and
unfold itself, till it reaches its culmination
in superconscious Samâdhi, the highest state
of Bliss.

*   *   *

53. Prânâyâma should be practised with
closed eyes. Instead of meditating then on
the form of the Chosen Ideal, direct your
attention to the breathing exercises, keeping
the required numbers by the Japa of your

Mantra, counting on the fingers of the left hand, in the usual way. These processes should be learnt from the Guru. While inhaling, think that you are drawing within yourself purity, compassion, strength, courage and other godly virtues; and while exhaling, think that you are ejecting from within all imperfections, such as evil thoughts, impurity, narrowness, envy and sinful tendencies.

* * *

54. If you are unable to meditate upon the form of your Chosen Ideal as dwelling within you in the lotus of the heart, you can meditate upon Him, instead, as seated on a lotus or a throne in front of you. The first method is of course the more commendable and the best, because it enables one to hold and see Him in the inmost recesses of one's heart or being. In the other method, He has to be thought of as existing outside. So, gradually, by continuous effort, try to see and think of Him as existing within. For the more one loves another, the more does one desire to keep and hold him close—in the heart of one's heart. "O my mind, let thee and

me alone see Him, and none else!"

55. If you are not able to practise Japa and meditation seated in the prescribed posture, for long periods in the morning and evening, you may do so at other times also, seated or resting in an easy posture, or even reposing in bed if you are not well. Or you may practise sitting up in bed in the small hours of the morning, if you do not feel tired or sleepy. But usually the mind is brought under control much better if Japa and meditation are done properly on a seat, according to the usual directions. You can also practise mentally repeating the Mantra without keeping count of the number, while walking, travelling in a conveyance, or doing some work, in the way of remembrance or recollection of God. But do not meditate at this time, for there is a risk of accident if you are unmindful of your surroundings. Time is invaluable; life is short and uncertain; do not waste a single moment.

56. Merits and defects combine to make a man. Everybody has both, either more,

or less, of one or the other. Instead of
searching for the faults and omissions of
others, rather look for your own. Magnify
the good qualities of others and your own
defects. Minimise the faults of others and
your own good qualities. Be like the bee
which is attracted by flowers, and not like
the fly which sits on sores and filth. Indulging in carping criticism of others or
idle gossip is harmful to Self-culture.

*　　　*　　　*

57. Only an Incarnation of God can be
free from faults and imperfections and
endowed with all the blessed qualities.
The conduct and dealings even of a man
of Realisation, of a highly advanced and
revered spiritual teacher, or of a fully
qualified Guru, may not be entirely without defects or imperfections, errors of
judgment or lack of proper understanding
of some sort or other. But their excep-
tional merits predominate to such an extent
that even their defects and eccentricities
often serve as embellishments to their
character and make them all the more
lovable. Besides, leaving apart these exalted personages, the eye of love does

not see the ugliness or blemishes of persons
who are loved or adored.

*   *   *

58. One cannot progress in the spiritual
world without sincere devotion and faith
in the Guru. Never doubt or disbelieve
the words of the Guru; know them to be
as sacred as the words of the Vedas or
scriptures. If you want to realise Truth,
try to follow implicitly the advice of the
Guru. Know that you have no other such
well-wisher as your Guru, either here or
hereafter. Steadfastly following the path
that he has pointed out to you is rendering
him true Seva, or service. That pleases him
the most.

*   *   *

59. In the beginning, Japa should be
practised slowly, distinctly uttering the
Mantra mentally. That takes time at first,
and it may not be possible to repeat the
Mantra more than two or three thousand
times in an hour, to start with. As practice increases it can be said more quickly.
Then, in course of time, one can easily
repeat the Mantra even eight or ten
thousand times in an hour. Try at the

time of Japa to concentrate the mind only
on the Mantra and the Chosen Ideal
signified by it.

* * *

60. The Guru cannot make you realise
the Truth unless you try hard for it yourself. The Guru can show you the way;
can remove your doubts and difficulties,
and correct your mistakes; can warn you
if you go astray; can put you back on the
right track; and can even take you some
distance along it, holding you by the
hand. But the walking you have to do
yourself—he cannot carry you to the goal
on his shoulders. The path is long and
difficult, no doubt; but it will not do if
for that reason you sit down in the middle
of the way, saying that it is beyond your
power to proceed further, or if you get
frightened, or give up hope. You cannot
stand still. You have either to go forward
or fall back. If you fall back, you will per-
force lose what you have already gained.
The more you go forward, the easier will
the path become. Courage and strength
will come, and you will get joy.

* * *

61. No amount of help is of any avail if there is no substance within oneself. Of what use is watering and weeding if the seeds have been sown in barren and stony soil? But as bad soil can be improved by various methods and made to yield good crops, even so can worldly-minded people attain the Supreme Goal if they follow the instructions of the Guru with simple faith, steadfastness and perseverance. Life will then become full of bliss and sweetness.

*	*	*

62. Onward! Onward! Do not look this way or that. Do not pay the slightest heed to psychic phenomena like the seeing of light or vision, etc. As you continue practising meditation, varieties of such occult experiences may come of themselves, and you may see all manner of supernatural things and also derive some joy from them. But do not stick there; for in that case you will never be able to progress much further. Always keep your whole attention fixed on the Ideal; and let your sole desire and aim be how to increase your devotion and love for God, how to merge your inind in Him, and how to gain

direct realisation of Him in this life.

* * *

63. Addiction to Siddhis and Bibhutis (occult and superhuman powers) leads men into the bondage of Maya and delusion through the temptation of enjoyment, and drags them down from the Ideal. The craving for these powers is not only a great obstacle to the realisation of God but it also gradually debases and ruins a person. Occult powers do not bring forth love of God nor lead to salvation. At best, they bring name and fame, and the enjoyments of desired objects in this world; and to satisfy these desires, mostly unholy, one does not even shrink from ruining others. Hence, true Bhaktas shun these powers like poison.

* * *

64. Our prayers are often mere words of mouth—lip-deep; we do not pray from the heart—that is why they bear no fruit. Our prayers are sure to be fulfilled if they come straight from the heart. When you feel that you are not deriving any result whatever by practising Japa and meditation, then search within to find out

the defects—the cracks and the holes
through which all the water of the vessel
is leaking out—and try to mend them.
Japa and meditation cannot transform or
work changes in the personality of an individual if strong attachment to the world
—to sense-objects, to lust and gold—remains.
But do not for that reason give up practising Japa and meditation regularly; you are
sure to get desired results in time. Worldly
pleasures will gradually appear to be insubstantial and insipid; love and devotion to
God will increase and you will find joy in
Him alone.

*　　*　　*

65. Our desire for Mukti or Liberation,
is mere pretence; it is not real and sincere.
If God were to appear before us and say:
"Here, I am granting you salvation, take
it!" we would then feel frightened and
be at our wit's ends, and cry out: "No,
no, I don't want Mukti at this instant;
what would happen to these near and
dear ones who depend upon me if I have
Mukti now? Give me Mukti after death!"
Do you not remember the story of
the old woodcutter? Exhausted by the

weight of his load, he was praying to Yama, the god of death, "O Lord, I can't bear it any longer, do release me!" When the god came and wanted to take him away, he said, "No, no, Lord, I called upon you just to help me lift this load of wood on to my head!" Similar is the plight of all human beings who are bound hand and foot to the world: they only want to escape from their miseries—not to have real Mukti.

* * *

66. What you intensely desire you are sure to get. If you really want God, you will find Him; if you pray to Him for worldly enjoyment, you will have that instead. But for either, you have to work; nothing can be acquired without toil and travail. What untold hardships people undergo for gaining worldly ends! They vigorously strive day and night with body, mind and soul, even foregoing food or sleep, for the sake of wife and children, for money, for property and possessions, for name and fame. There is no respite even for a moment, no escape; yet they do not get all they want, for there is no end

to their hopes and desires. If you could
strive in that way for God, you would
surely realise Him. Rejecting gold and
jewels, we are satisfied with bits of glass!
We receive blows again and again, yet we
are not brought to our senses. Such is the
illusion of Mahâmâyâ (Mother of cosmic
illusion). Realisation of God is difficult,
but it can become easy when a new turn or
direction is given to the trend or tendency
of the mind and it is wholly directed towards it. But he alone can do this, upon
whom the grace of the Mother descends.

* * *

67. It is certainly true that the desired
object cannot be had without toil. Little
children alone can get their wants satisfied without striving, for they know that
their mother understands all their needs.
They know nothing except the mother.
The mother gives whatever is needed and
whenever it is needed; they do not have
to think about it for themselves. One has
to become exactly like a child in spiritual
life. When the child is hungry, it cries,
and immediately the mother, leaving all
other work, comes and takes it in her lap

and suckles it. So you see, even the baby
has to cry to make its want known. Similarly, the devotee has also to call upon the
name of God, feel acutely his separation
from Him, and with tears pray yearningly
for the love of God. He does not care for
or look at anything else that might be given
to him. He wants God alone—not His
Divine powers, not even the bliss and
splendour of heaven. Wealth and riches are
no longer any attraction. Sang Râmprasâd,
the poet-devotee of Bengal:

" O Mother, of what use to me is
                        paltry wealth?
Who is crying for Thy riches?
If Thou givest any other treasure,
                        O Târâ,
It will lie uncared-for in a corner
                        of the room.
But if Thou givest Thy Lotus Feet
                        that dispel fear,
I shall keep them on the lotus seat of
                        my heart."

*   *   *

68. The essential thing is to bring the
mind under control. If you cannot do

that, nothing is of any use at all. As the
saying goes:

"Even if the grace of the three—the
　　Guru, Krishna (the Lord) and the
　　Vaishnava (devotee)—is obtained,
The Jiva lacking the grace of the
　　one, becomes nothing but dust and
　　ashes."

This 'one' is the mind. If the mind is
conquered, the world can be conquered.
All spiritual practice and discipline are for
that alone—the conquest of the mind.
Sri Ramakrishna used to sing a song, a
couplet of which is:

"The montore (Mantra) which I know,
　　that I have given unto you.
That is the Mantra by which I save
　　myself and others in danger; now,
　　*mon tore.**

*　　　*　　　*

69. A saintly Guru gives only such · a

---

* Here is a pun on the word, *montore*, (colloquial
for 'Mantra') and *mon tore* meaning in Bengali,
'your mind'. So it means—it all depends upon your
mind, whether it accepts and profits by it or not.
(Really, this stanza cannot be effectively translated in
English.)

Mantra as has been handed down in the line of Gurus; and repeating which, the Yogis and Rishis (seers) have attained Perfection. He does not impart any fanciful product of his imagination to his disciple. One should never lose faith in the Mantra or hold it as trivial. If long and methodical practice of Japa with the Mantra does not make the mind one-pointed or purified, know that the Mantra is not at fault, but that the reason lies in your own shortcomings. If you do not try to mend these, of what avail will the mere lip-practice of Japa be, or changing your Guru and becoming the disciple of another? One has to do Japa with both mind and tongue at one.

*　　　　*　　　　*

70. Know the Mantra to be the source of great power and the very essence of the Chosen Ideal. One has to catch hold of the gross to reach the subtle; and through the subtle, one attains to the super-subtle, which is beyond the reach of mind and speech.

*　　　　*　　　　*

71. The great secret of meditation is to

transform the ego-consciousness into the
Supreme Consciousness, which is the true
nature of the individual soul. The process
is to place the Supreme Self, or the Personal
God (Brahman with qualities), deep within
the heart, or the inmost being, of the individual self, to try repeatedly to free the
mind of all attachments to sense objects by
prayers, by discrimination of good and evil,
and by the repetition of the Mantra. Thus
the mind becomes more and more absorbed,
and when that attitude ripens and attains
its fullest development so that it flows like
an unbroken stream of oil, then only will
the mind be truly merged in the luminous
and blissful form and idea of the Chosen
Ideal, which is Pure Love, Existence and
Bliss—the Brahman Absolute. That state is
called Bhâva, the blessed mood of spiritual
ecstasy, or Samâdhi, the superconscious
state of oneness with Divinity.

* * *

72. If one forms the habit of practising
Japa and meditation steadfastly every day,
it develops into a sort of craving in course
of time. When meditation deepens, one
gets a feeling of intoxication, as it were,

which endures for some time afterwards.
One feels exalted. So you should not get
up or engage in worldly talk immediately
after meditation. There is no wish to talk
at that time. One feels disturbed and pained
in doing so. Try to make that mood last
as long as you can.

*   *   *

73. As drunkards or drug-addicts feel
intensely miserable and find everything out
of joint if they do not get their drink or
drug at the accustomed time, so do the
Sâdhakas (aspirants) feel on that day when
for any reason they fail to do Japa and
meditation as usual. So it is also with everything, more or less, when a particular habit
is formed, either good or bad.

*   *

74. "Do we worldly people have any
hope of salvation?" Why not? Certainly
there is every hope. Is God for the Sannyâsins alone? Everybody is His child.
Who can live entirely out of the world?
We Sannyâsins, too, have our worldly
concerns. We also have to think for the
good of others and feel concerned to
hear of their troubles and miseries; we

have to think of the welfare of the Sannyâsins of the monastery and our worldwide organisation (Math and Mission); we
have to think about the growth and ex-
pansion of the work of the Master—the
dissemination of his ideas and ideals; and,
though not last, we are deeply afflicted
with tales of heart-rending woes and sufferings of our diseased, homeless, hunger-
stricken, destitute fellow-beings, as a result
of widespread famines, floods, and epi-
demics, and to think of ways and means of
mitigating them. But there is a world of
difference between thinking for one's self
and for others. One belongs to Mâyâ or
Avidyâ (ignorance). The other is of Vidyâ
(knowledge). There is no harm in remaining in the world, but take care
that you are not of the world—that it is
not the be-all and end-all of your life.
Remain in the world and fulfil all your
duties and obligations, but see that you
have the idea of renunciation, of non-agent-
ship—"I am not the doer"—of non-attachment, ever-present within yourself.

* * *

75. Know the world to be a long

dream. As long as it lasts, continue to do your duty, with the consciousness that the world is relatively true, for practical purposes. But at the same time firmly hold on to the conviction that God alone is the only True and Eternal Reality, and that there is no final happiness, peace or Mukti until He is realised. After having this rare privilege of human birth and the opportunity for attaining true knowledge, life and everything else are in vain if you do not try to realise Him.

* * *

76. External renunciation is not of much consequence, so long as the world fills the mind and there is attachment and craving for sense-objects. Wherever you may fly to, renouncing merely outwardly, whether to the forests or to the mountain caves, the world will follow you there also, deceiving you and tempting you under many guises, and will create fresh bondages for you. Householder or Sannyàsin, whatever you may be, if you do not constantly keep your eye on the Ideal and have a firm grip on it, a fall is inevitable; and none will be able to save you.

77. Be always alert. Never believe your mind for a moment. However spiritually high may be the state you have reached, do not be over-confident of having conquered the senses, for a fall is still possible. In subtle ways, evil may try to beguile you by assuming sometimes the form of virtue, sometimes the form of compassion, sometimes the form of friendship, to bring you under its power. In the long run, you may find that unknowingly you have lost yourself. And by the time you come to know it, it may be well-nigh impossible to turn back.

*   *   *

78. As a rule, it is preferable to marry and be a householder, because this is also one of the four Ashramas, or preparatory stages of life, one of the paths of self-improvement. But if a Brahmacharin (initiate who has taken the vow of continence) or an ordained Sannyâsin becomes a slave to lust and gold, he commits sin and forfeits both this world and the next. Those who have renounced the world, as also widows, should keep to their vows of life-long continence, and never consciously vio-

late them. Those who are unable to do
that should not hesitate to marry, both for
their own good as well as the good of
others, since this is permitted by the scriptures. "Better to marry than to burn," says
St Paul in the Bible.

*　　　*　　　*

79. It is very necessary for everybody,
man or woman, to qualify in some branch
of learning, craft or technical profession
which will enable him to earn an indepen-
dent livelihood. Dependence on others is a
miserable state; it makes life unbearable—
what to speak of devoting oneself, in such
circumstances, to spiritual exercises and religious acts, however earnestly one may
desire to do!

*　　　*　　　*

80. Whole-hearted practice of the Mantra
imparted by the Guru and an ardent effort
to follow his instructions in the details of
life, are the Guru's only real remuneration
(Guru-dakshinâ), and are the best means
to gain his affection and blessings and to
attain spiritual perfection.

*　　　*　　　*

81. As the father desires to be surpassed

6

by his son, so also does the Guru wish to be surpassed by his disciple. The father wants his son, and the Guru his disciple, to be greater than he.

*   *   *

82. God Himself is the Supreme Guru, the Guru of the guru. He it is who is the Doer. The man-Guru is merely His instrument—the vehicle through which His power is transmitted to the disciple.

*   *   *

83. The qualified Guru imparts to the disciple, through initiation by the Mantra, the deepest secret truth which he himself has realised by his own spiritual practices. Do not attempt to judge or value him by the foot-rule of practical reason. This would be like the green-grocer who priced the diamond at exactly nine seers of eggplants—and not a single one more! These are not matters of argument or disputation, but are subtle mysterious truths not grasped by the intellect. They can only be comprehended if one goes on doing spiritual practices with firm faith in the instructions of the Guru. Then, veil after veil will be

lifted, and the light of Truth will shine in all its glory.

*　　　*　　　*

84. Practise Japa and meditation every day, at least for some time. When you fail to do so, ask yourself: Is it want of time, or want of heart? You manage to find time for every kind of work, however trivial it may be; and yet you do not get time for practising Japa and meditation for an hour or so! As water is necessary to quench thirst and food to satisfy hunger, as breathing is necessary for life, Japa and meditation, prayer and spiritual practices are just as necessary, if not more so, for the realisation of the Higher Truth. A feeling of wanting Him has to be created. This will come gradually through daily practice, and power will be accumulated by it.

*　　　*　　　*

85. There are many who say to the Guru after initiation, "We shall not be able to do anything. We are now free, having placed all responsibility upon you." This is just an excuse for evading one's own responsibility, and for not wishing to do anything. Is spirituality so easily acquired?

Is it so cheap? "As is the idea, so is the attainment." Realisation is commensurate with the depth and intensity of thought and action. Can all responsibility be shifted to the Guru by mere word of mouth? One has to surrender oneself completely, by sacrificing one's little ego. That is achieved by long practice. You run about day and night and work ceaselessly, even giving up food and sleep, to earn a few paltry coins. But when it comes to the matter of acquiring spiritual knowledge and devotion, you say, "We shall not be able to do anything!" How absurd, indeed! Truth can only be realised if one devotes oneself whole-heartedly to spiritual practice to the best of one's ability, day after day, month after month, year after year. There is no other path than this. There is no other way to Mukti.

*   *   *

86. No one can take upon himself anybody else's burden of sin, not even the Guru. It is a great mistake to suppose that the Guru has taken upon his shoulders the whole burden of your sins by initiating you. Only the Incarnations of God can

and, in fact, do that, because they are, verily, an unconditioned ocean of mercy. They come down specially for the purpose of delivering sinners and the afflicted. No sin can touch God; yet, because of His assuming the human body, sins of those who take refuge in Him attack Him in the shape of diseases and cause Him suffering. A sin committed, can be atoned for only by a poignant feeling of repentance within, and by leading a holy life after having given up all sinful actions. The fire of Self-knowledge alone can burn up all tendency to sin.

* * *

87. People consider religion a thing for which no training or trouble is necessary, as if it is unclaimed property lying on the path, which has merely to be picked up! Everyone comes forward to give his opinion or prescription in regard to religion and considers himself an adept, an all-knowing person, without studying the scriptures or going through spiritual practices of any kind! To master any secular knowledge, one has to study for many years under a proficient teacher. The idea that spiritual

knowledge can be acquired and the subtlest
truths of religion comprehended in life
without very strenuous training or discipline, is simply ridiculous.

*   *   *

88. Many complain only a short time
after initiation, "Why is it that the mind
is not getting quiet, that we are not able
to meditate properly? Please do something to make the mind calm." Is it easy
to have a quiet mind, or the faculty of
diving deep into meditation? The mind
has a natural outgoing tendency under the
influence of Samskâras (habits, tendencies
and impressions) and attachment to sense-
objects accumulated in previous lives. Consequently, it always seeks to possess and
enjoy those objects. There is no short-
cut to make this restless mind quiet,
except by repeated effort and renunciation. One has to practise Japa and
meditation with patience and constancy—
day after day, month after month, nay,
year after year—in accordance with the
method prescribed by the Guru, and, at the
same time, to try to develop non-attachment to worldly objects. The more the

craving for sense-objects decreases, the more the love and devotion for your Chosen Ideal will grow. The more you realise Him to be nearer and dearer than your own dear ones, the more will the mind automatically become calm and quiet. Then meditation will also deepen, and you will have joy and peace. Instead of being in a hurry for quick results, one must stick to spiritual practices like Sri Ramakrishna's hereditary peasant, who goes on tilling his soil even if his crops fail year after year.

* * *

89. When you go to visit a temple of God or a Sannyâsin, you should not go without an offering. Take with you at least a pice or two worth of fruits or sweets, or at least a few flowers.

* * *

90. Do not give way to depression by wailing and continuously brooding over the trials and tribulations, oppressions, strained relations, misunderstandings and quarrels, and such other mental disturbances, which are inevitable in worldly life. It is of no

use. On the contrary, the more you ponder over them or discuss them with others, the greater proportions they will assume; they will increase tenfold. You will completely lose your peace of mind, and life will become unbearable. Try to put up with difficulties as best as you can. Words give rise to more words. If, therefore, anybody says something unpleasant or unjust to you, it is better to ignore it and keep quiet. The dumb have no enemies. The Master used to say, "He who endures, prevails, he who does not is destroyed." Sweet words, sweet dealings, forbearance, service and love—in the long run these triumph over all ills of life. Even wild animals become submissive by kind treatment. Examine yourself and resolve firmly in your mind to mend your defects, even if you fail again and again; lay all your troubles before God; weep and pray to Him from your heart to remove all your faults and mistakes. It is vain, nay, madness, to try to mend others; we should mend ourselves. Have no ill-feeling towards anybody. To one who is good, the whole world is good. If you cannot do this, the blame is your own and you have to suffer the consequence.

* * *

91. Attachment, or the sense of ownership, in relation to objects or individuals is the root cause of all the bondage in the world. The Jnâni, or man of Knowledge, does not love anybody personally, nor does he want others to love or be attached to him personally. Because he is free himself, he does not want anybody to be in bondage through the ties of personal attachment to him. Because he sees his own Self, God, in all, his Prema (love), is universal—is the same for all beings. There is no physical or sensual touch in his Prema, no trace of lust, no infatuation for physical beauty. The Jnâni is truly the real lover, and the true lover of God is a Jnâni.

* * *

92. Renunciation, love of God and purity are the means of realising Him. They are inter-related as the limbs to the body: if one is present, the other two are also there. God, whose nature is love and purity, cannot be attained without aversion for worldly objects, without love for all beings and

the feeling that they are one's very own;
nor without external and internal purity
of body, mind and speech. If one constantly strives with diligence to maintain
an unbroken flow of pure thought within,
all impure thoughts and tendencies will
fly away. The character will be so transformed that evil thoughts and deeds, feelings of malice or envy, become impossible.
Such a man radiates a power that turns
evil-doers into good persons. The worst
sinner, at his touch, becomes religious and
truthful, even the atheist is converted into
a devotee of God, and men tormented by
the afflictions of the world, find abiding
peace.

* * *

93. As sin and venereal poison in the
blood cannot be kept suppressed, even so
Love and purity cannot be kept hidden.
Can fire be covered by a cloth? However much a person who has nothing to
call his own, who makes no distinction
between friend and foe, hides himself from
public gaze, the whole world becomes illu-
minated by the light of his Knowledge
and is flooded by the tidal wave of his

Divine Love. He is blessed indeed who takes refuge in and receives the grace of such a Knower of Brahman.

* * *

94. Youth is the best time for the practice of spirituality. If at that time one can accumulate enough spiritual power through strenuous endeavour, one can pass the rest of his life in comparative security from the fear of slipping down, and in happiness and peace. No matter how many difficulties and dangers come, he remains unshaken. Unless you build up your character in youth, it is no longer possible to do so afterwards. Do not waste even a single moment in idleness or fruitless activity. "My health is not good!" —"I do not find time!"—Such are the excuses. They are all nonsense. If meals and recreation, sleep and all other daily activities are controlled and regulated, the body and mind will keep vigorous and cheerful, and much more work can be had out of them. Moreover, the quality of work will also improve, and one will find that one has sufficient time for spiritual

practice or any other work.

*　　　　*　　　　*

95. One feels neither cheerful in mind
nor strong in body if one eats indiscrimi-
nately whatever one gets or whenever one
gets it, and lives a disordered existence,
freely indulging in lust and other passions.
So much burden is unreasonably laid upon
the body and mind by reckless living that
the body breaks down at last and becomes
incapable even of physical exertion. After
gormandizing all sorts of food, half the
energy of the body is wasted in digesting
it; even eight to ten hours' sleep will not
make up for this. Whatever energy remains is also liable to be frittered away
in vain pursuits and idle gossip. Consequently, little or nothing remains for practising meditation and Japa, nor is there
even any inclination for it. As soon as
such persons sit for spiritual practice, they
begin to yawn and doze. If things go on
like this, what great work can ever be
done? Let alone practices of spirituality
and doing of good works, it is not even
possible for such a person to be a practical
man of the world. What a pity that such

a rare thing as human life should be wasted away in this fashion! If even human virtues cannot be gained in human life, which holds the promise of Divinity, then what is the difference between it and the life of a brute?

*   *   *

96. A beginner in spiritual life should ever be awake and alert, so that the mind, as yet unripe, may not lead him into bondage through unwitting attachment to persons or things. And it should be remembered that this stage of a beginner does not mean only the brief period when spiritual exercises have just been begun. Ten or twelve years' practice of Japa and meditation does not necessarily make an aspirant the possessor of a higher degree of spirituality. The first stage may continue for many years, or even for life, until something is directly realised. It lasts according to the difference in degree of eagerness and effort on the part of different individuals. This perception of Truth is the beginning of real religion or spirituality. Any religious rituals, ceremonies, austerities and discipline performed before that,

are mere preparations and aids for entering the realm of the Spirit.

* * *

97. It is seen in the case of those who have begun to do spiritual practices and Japa and meditation that the more they try to concentrate the mind on the Ishta, the more vehemently the mind rebels and runs after all sorts of irrelevant nonsense. One wonders, "Why did I have no such trouble before? I used to be able to apply myself to my occupations with a fairly steady mind. Why can't I do so now?" The reason is, that the mind formerly used to be engaged in external pursuits and be attracted towards sense-objects by its very nature, and so there was no conflict. No sooner is an attempt made to control the mind, to draw it away from unsubstantial, external objects and to make it look within, by discrimination between the real and the unreal, than it rebels. The force of a river increases a hundredfold if an attempt is made to dam it. And if that mighty force —if the tremendous power that is generated thereby—is turned to some useful and

desired purpose, a thousandfold result is obtained.

* * *

98. Success in any matter is achieved by diligence and effort. Try again and again if you fail. If you do not succeed even after diligent effort, know that you have not put forth the requisite amount of effort. Everything will be pliant and easy of attainment if you only really try more and more and never give up. Gradually the habit will be formed and will become part of your own nature.

* * *

99. God has not really left us in want of anything; the want is in the mind only. Happiness and misery are in the mind, and not outside. "As is the mental conception so is the attainment." We get what we seek.

* * *

100. Freedom is supreme happiness. Dependence is extreme misery. But dependence on God is true independence. The servant of God is the master of Creation. One cannot become a servant of God unless one gives up slavery to the six pas-

sions, namely, lust, anger, greed, infatuation, pride and envy.

*   *   *

101. A man's bondage as well as his salvation are in his own hands. Yet, knowingly and in spite of being warned, we put ourselves into bondage, created by our own folly or delusive imagination and suffer miserably. The plight of the world-bound soul is like that of the man who encircling his arms round a post holds some popped-rice in his joined palms and vainly strains at eating it. He can neither eat it nor let loose his palms lest it is blown away.

*   *   *

102. The Tantra says, "That person goes to hell who regards his Guru as a mere human being, who holds the holy Mantra of his Chosen Ideal as mere words, or looks upon the images of gods and goddesses as mere stone or clay." The meaning is that if, owing to want of faith and devotion, a person entertains such perverted and materialistic notions contrary to scriptural injunctions, as stated above— he not only blocks the path of his spiritual

progress, but also courts his own ruin.

* * *

103. Those who always remember and think of God, repeat His name in the midst of all their work and activity, and know Him to be their only resource and refuge, never miss Him when beset with dangers and calamities. Even at the last moment, thoughts of Him will make them oblivious of the pangs of death, will drive away their attachment to the world, to men and money, and the mind will be wholly fixed in Him, enjoying His Presence. Such a consummation comes to those only who are no more to be born and to die in this world. By repeated practice of Remembrance and feeling His Presence, these become part of their very nature.

* * *

104. The more you strengthen the conviction that the Holy Name and the Person named, are one, the more you will feel His presence in the heart of your being.

* * *

105. The world is said to be that place where none is one's own and where none even owns himself! So ephemeral is our

mundane existence!

* * *

106. One who is a friend to himself is a friend to the world, and the whole world also is a friend to him. "This self is the friend of oneself, and this self is the enemy of oneself," says Sri Krishna in the Gita (VI. 5). That is to say, pure mind is the cause of one's Mukti and the impure mind —that of bondage.

* * *

107. In this ever-changing evanescent world, union coexists with separation, prosperity with adversity, happiness with misery, fortune with misfortune, enjoyment with disease, property with strife. Each follows the other like a shadow that passes. Knowing this and experiencing this, why do men still get entangled in such a world through the lure of phantom happiness? The immediacy of the pleasure derived from the enjoyment of sense-objects is the undoing of man. Even a grain of nominal pleasure makes one forget the pains of miseries suffered a million times!

* * *

108. One can escape from the clutches of misery only if one always thinks over the ultimate result that his acts may bring. Who can remove the misery of one who fails to learn even by repeated experience? Who can awaken one who is feigning sleep? The true fruition of human life is reached by taking the steps necessary to avoid coming back to this world and undergoing endless sufferings, by being born again and again.

*   *   *

109. No work can ever be done and nothing can ever be successfully accomplished, if one sits idle and waits for what fate or luck may bring. Moreover, such an attitude makes a man unmanly and Tâmasic (inert) and debases him altogether. Men commit mistakes or fail because of their own faults, and they put the whole blame on evil fate or luck or stars! A person trips or slips through his own carelessness, but blames the ground! All achievement usually depends upon one's own effort. If there be anything called fate which is felt to be an obstacle to the realisation of the aim of life, it has to be

overcome by rousing with self-effort the innate strength that lies dormant within everyone. Only then are you a Man. If you do that, you will find that fate also will be favourable to you. If fate alone were all-powerful, there could be no such things as talking of right or wrong, virtue or vice, or the power of the Spirit. Men are not stocks and stones. "Fate alone is causing me to do everything, I am not responsible for my acts; I am being helplessly driven along by it."—If this be the mental attitude, no man can ever rise, or hope to reach Mukti, or salvation. Remember, it is nothing but degrading for a man to think himself weak and at the mercy of unseen Powers; it pushes him down more and more into the mire.

*   *   *

110. Only he who has succeeded in merging his own will in the Will of God has a right to say, "I am being irresistibly driven to do all this; I am the machinery and He is the Operator." That can be done only by a devotee of the highest type, who knows nothing else but God. He never takes a false step even unwittingly; no

wicked deed can ever be done by him; his heart remains filled with irrepressible strength and inspiration and is never assailed by despair or depression; and he is moved neither by happiness nor misery. He always has the feeling of "Not I, not I, but Thou, but Thou, my Lord." Gain and loss, victory and defeat, honour and dishonour, have all become the same to him.

*   *   *

111. When some work has to be done, you should be full of activity, setting yourself to it with all your heart and soul. Do not pay the slightest heed to obstacles and hindrances, if they turn up, however insuperable they may seem to be. You will then find that those very obstacles and hindrances will actually help you in some way or other. Is it always possible to have a favourable atmosphere after one's own heart? The person who thinks that he will devote himself to the worship of God with a carefree mind, after having completed all his duties and settled all his family affairs satisfactorily, fares like the fool who goes to bathe in the sea, but frightened by its dreadful waves, thinks he

will go into the water only after the waves
have subsided a little and the sea become
calm. That never comes about, even if he
sits on the beach till the last day of his life.
There will always be waves in the sea. One
should boldly jump into the sea, bathe
fighting with the waves, and get through
with it. In the same way, in this sea of the
world, one must call on God, do spiritual
practices and worship Him, fighting all
along with the waves. But your hope of
realisation will never be fulfilled if you sit
down hugging your knees in despair, and
wait for the right moment and the opportune circumstances to turn up.

*　　*　　*

112. Many express eagerness to become
monks of the Ramakrishna Order, with a
view to avoiding their worldly responsibilities, or when they have failed to secure a
job, or have suffered from chronic poverty,
want and all manner of troubles and
miseries, and have been frustrated at every
step in their undertakings. Nowadays, it
has become a sort of fashion, as it were, to
become a Sannyâsin! Is it easy to have
true Vairâgyam, or aversion for worldly

desires and passions, and to become a real Sannyâsin, or man of renunciation? One has to acquire fitness for that life while living in the world by preparing the ground with spiritual disciplines, so as to train oneself at least to some extent in the habit of non-attachment to objects, unconcern and selflessness. Otherwise, the sudden outburst of new love soon fizzles out like a fire made of palm leaves. The days are passed in laziness and the mind gravitates towards personal happiness and comfort, name and fame. One then sits for an hour or so and somehow gets done with Japa and meditation as a matter of drudgery, or forced labour. "Today I am not keeping well,"—"Yesterday I did not find time because of other work"—some excuse or other of this sort crops up. It is often seen that after getting quit of worldly worries and obstacles, and living the life of renunciation in ease and contentment, one thinks, "I have now got what I wanted; there is no reason to be in a hurry now; it will do well enough if I call on God at my leisure and convenience." The original spirit and fervour have vanished, and the mind by and by takes a downward course.

*   *   *

113. People from outside viewing the Belur Math (monastery) think, "How well the monks live! Such a beautiful place on the bank of the Ganga! Such nice buildings and temples, and no dearth of money! There is no anxiety, no worry! The life of the Sâdhus is a round of feasts and festivities! They do a little work of the Master at regular hours, and a little study or practice of Japa and meditation in their own way, and do as they please the rest of the time! What a free and happy life!" These critics little know how much work the monks of the Order have to do day and night; what stringent rules and regulations they have to observe; what a variety of arduous service they have to render constantly; how caring not for their health and scorning their own lives they have to be always ready for any emergency. They little know that these Sâdhus (monks) have to face death cheerfully in many a dangerous undertaking for the relief and deliverance of the afflicted

and the distressed—how giving up their
life of intense Sâdhanâ or spiritual practices, and even throwing away their own
salvation, they dedicate their lives to the
Service of humanity, looking upon man as
the living God. The monastic member who
does not carry out the bidding of the Order,
or who tries to shirk it by proffering
excuses, or who goes away and lives as he
pleases—such misguided people, following
their own whims, sink down. The road of
their progress becomes barred and they
gradually fall from their Ideal.

* * *

114. A householder devotee, endowed
with faith and earnestness, though unable
to do much spiritual practice, is a thousand
times better than the Sannyâsin who has
fallen from the Ideal. The former is striving his utmost, according to his ability, to
advance on the path of spiritual progress,
and is praying to God with a yearning
heart for liberation from his intolerable
bondage. An intense longing for renunciation grows in his heart as he keeps on
fighting with diverse obligations of duty
and obstacles and hindrances which con-

stantly face him in his worldly life. His heart hungers and pines for God-vision, and thus the desire to realise Him by breaking the bondage and renouncing the world is steadily intensified. This longing quickens the power of the Spirit within. God comes to his help. He is the Inner Guide, and knowing the devotee's plight, He gradually removes the impediments in the way to his salvation. The truth is, that unless the desire for renunciation comes from the heart, nothing—neither Love, nor Liberation, nor Knowledge—can be gained.

*   *   *

115. Many think, "Of what use will it be if I take up the path of Work or of Service to humanity? Let me rather try first to realise God by following the path of Yoga and meditation day and night." Is that possible? If you try it for a few months or so, you will come to understand that it is not practicable. How will the mind be purified unless you work for the good of others? Does the mind become calm and peaceful before it is purified? And if the mind be not still, is it easy to meditate or

to concentrate it on the Ideal? It is through work that one gets the true test and measure of himself; one then discovers the limitations of one's powers and abilities. It is through work only that one comes to know how many and what are the defects and weaknesses in the mind, how strong is the attraction for and attachment to worldly objects, how much selfishness and egotism and how much patience and forbearance are there, and whether these are gradually increasing or decreasing. And it is only through the performance of work and Service that the easiest and the surest remedy for these defects is to be found. If the habit of discrimination between the real and unreal, and self-introspection and self-analysis be cultivated, the mind gradually becomes pure and desireless, egoistic feeling is destroyed and the heart becomes filled with Divine Love. Then, one does not look upon work as work, and far from being a cause of bondage work becomes a means of Liberation. That is to say, work is then transformed into worship; no difference is felt between work and worship of God, between service of man as divine and devotion to Him. That alone is true Bhakti, or love of God. And the most natural way to gain that, is to follow the path of Karma Yoga, work without attachment.

116. Supreme love of God cannot be acquired without the attainment of Knowledge also—that is to say, without realisation that my Chosen Ideal, God, is in all beings and individuals, that the animate and inanimate worlds have no separate existence apart from Him. The feeling of identity, or oneness, between the Supreme Self and the animate and inanimate worlds, as well as the inner-self, is itself Supreme Love and Supreme Knowledge. But the two paths and the modes of spiritual practice pertaining to each, differ according to the respective bent of mind and qualifications of the aspirants. Persons qualified to tread exclusively the path of Knowledge are rare in the world; the path is also extremely arduous. For this reason, Bhakti mixed with Jnâna is preferable.

117. In the path of Knowledge

(Jnâna), the existence of everything has to be negated right from the start— "Not this, not this, I am not this, not that. Nothing whatever that I see, hear, or perceive is I. I am not the body, nor the mind, nor the sense-organs; it is not I that experiences sickness, sorrow, happiness or misery, heat and cold. The manifested universe—is altogether non-existent, that is, it has no existence in the three divisions of time—past, present and future —and hence is unreal. I am of the nature of the indivisible Existence-Knowledge-Bliss, the Supreme Brahman, the Supreme Self, the One without a second." Is it ever possible for an individual with the limitations of the body, ego, etc. to practise such a rigorous discipline? A thorn is pricking the flesh, or fire is burning it, still there is no feeling of pain! This is the final state of a man of perfect renunciation who is devoid of the least attachment to sense-objects, the state which is experienced in Nirvikalpa Samâdhi—the highest state of Superconsciousness beyond all modifications of the mind—the culmination of all spiritual practice and realisation. The Master used to say that the body does not last more than twenty-one days in that state.

*   *   *

118. The path of devotion, or Bhakti Yoga, is easy for all to tread for the reason that this does not require the killing of the senses or uprooting the natural urges and desires; one needs only to give them a new turn. Their tendencies, drives and energies are to be directed along new channels. This can be done by the line of least resistance. One has to withdraw the mind gently from sense-objects and point it God-ward. The way to do this is to get rid of desires by perceiving, with the help of discrimination and reason, the entirely evil character of lust, anger, greed and delusion, which are the causes of endless suffering and bondage; and also to realise that unless these passions are conquered, men have to be born and to die again and again, and their misery will not completely end, even in eternity. By these means the evil desires and proclivities not only lose their force gradually, but their irrepressible downward tendencies can, by the process

of sublimation, be led upward, and be converted into such tremendous forces of good that they flood life with an inexhaustible feeling of supreme bliss. If you crave for pleasure, thirst for the ecstasy of being in the blessed company of the Lord, who is All-Love! If you must be avaricious, covet the possession of the imperishable Supreme Treasure, which is God! If you must be infatuated with beauty, be enamoured of the Eternally Beautiful! If you have to be angry, be angry with Him for not revealing Himself to you! And so on in regard to pride and envy also, which keep you down to the trifles of life.

*　　*　　*

119. In the beginning one should follow the path of work and that of spiritual practices. Both are necessary. The one has to be done along with the other in harmonious combination. Have the firm conviction that the aim of both is the realisation of God. If in action that ideal is not kept steadily before the mind's eye, all manner of distractions and mental disturbances make their appearance, and one loses oneself in the mazes of work. Proper balance

must be studiously observed. It is the
same in regard to any other ideal of life.
For that reason, one should be always
awake and alert, should always discriminate between the real and the unreal, and
cultivate the habit of prayer. If this is
done, there will come a time, by the grace
of God, when no difference will be felt
between work and spiritual practice; everything done will then be transformed into
spiritual practice. But it is necessary for
a devout worker to go now and then on
pilgrimages, and to carry on spiritual practices and austerities intensively for some
time, say, a year or so, in a secluded place,
filled with the spirit of entire renunciation
and dependence on God. This makes the
body and mind refreshed, vigorous and
cheerful, brings self-confidence and reliance
on God, and builds up strength and an all-
round character.

*   *   *

120. Anyone who has been initiated can,
without exception, perform the worship of
his Chosen Ideal. Initiation purifies the
body. Do your worship (Pujâ) with profound devotion, knowing Him to be your

very own, and placing your entire faith in Him. Offer flowers, sandal-paste, garlands and sweets, as your heart desires. If the mind be absorbed in worship, it will easily become quiet, meditation will deepen and you will find great joy. There are no Do's and Don'ts in the worship actuated by love, no need for sacred texts, formulae, diagrams, genuflexions, particular gestures, or manipulation of fingers. The only requisites are faith, reverence and love. At the time of performing worship, think that your Chosen Ideal is really and lovingly accepting your offerings of flowers, fruits, sweets and other objects, however insignificant they may be. Food anointed with love and devotion is very sweet and dear to Him. He partook with extreme relish of the plain lowly fare of Bhakta Vidur, refusing the invitation of King Duryodhana. Whatever you eat, eat after offering it mentally to Him; know that to be consecrated food, the gift of His mercy. This destroys any spiritually harmful properties that may be attached to the food.

*   *   *

121. Sevâ (Service), Swâdhyāya (study

8

of scriptures), Sâdhanâ (spiritual practices),
Satya (Truth), Samyama (restraint)—these
five 'S' 's are the best means of Realisation.
Always practise them with diligence and
to the utmost of your ability.

* * *

122. The bad tendencies (Samskâras) of
this life and of the previous ones are annihilated and good tendencies formed and
strengthened by the steady and regular
practice of such daily duties as Pujâ,
Swâdhyâya, Service, Japa and meditation,
etc. As a result of this, spiritual practices
gradually become easy to perform, and the
mind, becoming pure and steady, is absorbed in the thought of God and ultimately
attains knowledge of Reality.

* * *

123. Unless one has an incentive derived
from some good tendencies or virtuous
work done in previous lives, one does not
have faith in religion or in God, nor feel
any inclination towards them. Even if such
faith or inclination be there as a result
of some extraordinary work of religious
merit, so many hindrances and obstructions make their appearance that it is ex-

tremely difficult to make rapid progress in
the religious path. But it will not do for
that reason to give up in despair. The
more firmly you resolve to overcome them,
the more will they fly from your path.
And not only so, but it may even happen
that those obstructions themselves will give
up their hostility and will be friendly and
helpful to you. The more you are afraid
to face obstacles and impediments, the more
will they try to frighten you and prove
stubborn.

*   *   *

124. Without good tendencies acquired
from the past life, one cannot properly
comprehend the scriptures and the instructions of the Guru. One may have attained
great heights in learning and intellectual-
ity, or in any other line; one may have
high position, name, fame and honour in
society; one may have an excellent business
head and be a multimillionaire; but in so
far as the subtle truths of the Spirit are
concerned, one may be as ignorant as a
baby, and may not easily understand even
the simplest things of religion. But if one
is truthful and has faith, simplicity and

love, and feels for the poor and the afflicted, one may be blessed, by the grace of God, with the company of holy persons and a competent Guru, and gain their favour. As a result of this, one acquires fitness for comprehending the subtle truths of religion.

* * *

125. Even if there are not many good past impressions, favourable ones can be created by virtue of constant effort, earnestness and practice. There is tremendous power in practice. Practice becomes firm and abiding if continued long and uninterruptedly with faith and devotion. Whatever you practise becomes in course of time your second nature. Then it is no longer necessary to exert yourself to accomplish a desired thing, for it is automatically done. If you constantly practise the remembrance of God, prayer, Japa and meditation, they then come out from the heart, without the exercise of any conscious will or effort, even while you are engaged in other work. The mind remains pointed that way, like the needle of a compass. Hence attachment to worldly objects disappears, and dangers and

calamities cannot ruffle the mind of such a person. Even at the moment of death the mind remains calm and absorbed in Him. Such a one has not to be born and to die again and again, as he becomes merged in the supreme state of Beatitude.

*   *   *

126. If you are able to establish God in your heart, by means of spiritual practice done with intense sincerity, discrimination, dispassion and love, you will realise Him, and see Him everywhere, within and without, and in all things. There remains no longer anything else in the universe for such a one to gain or to desire; his life is filled with bliss. This is the only true aim of human life. All else is nothing but chasing shadows.

*   *   *

127. Practise Japa and austerities with all your heart as much as you can. You should, however, have it firmly fixed in your mind that God can be realised solely through His grace*, and not as a result of

* Hari Maharaj (Swami Turiyananda) has beautifully and repeatedly made observations of this kind in his "Letters". The purport of them is given in this and in the three subsequent paragraphs.

your practising so much Japa and austerities. Spiritual practices are meant merely
for tiring the wings, so to speak. A bird
wants to rest as soon as its wings are tired.
After flying far out at sea, the bird discovers that there is no other resting-place
except the mast of a ship, and it perches
there. But unless the feeling that God is
the only refuge grows into an unshakable
conviction, no one can take shelter completely in Him and know Him to be his
All-in-all.

* * *

128. The true devotee never has a shop-
keeping attitude towards God. The idea of
bargaining with Him for Bhakti and Mukti
never enters his mind. He knows that God
is the ocean of unconditioned mercy, that
He will unquestionably bestow His grace by
virtue of His own character and nature.
One has, however, to do spiritual practices
to the best of one's ability, in order to
come finally to the inevitable conclusion
that nothing of all these practices is of any
slightest consequence, without His mercy.
So a devotee has sung:

"If it be Thy will, O Mother, to save me

by virtue of Thy own nature, then turn Thy gaze of mercy upon me! Otherwise, all such talk of finding Thee by practising Japa is like the Sângâ of ghost." Sângâ means marriage. What marriage can there be for ghosts? It is nonsense! Nobody has ever realised Him or will ever realise Him merely by the power of spiritual practices. The man of wisdom knows that the hope of attaining Him by means of spiritual practices is like "crossing the ocean by swimming".

* * *

129. Should one then give up spiritual practices and wait supinely in the hope of finding Him when His grace will descend by itself? Can one who is tormented with thirst, and whose heart yearns for Him, sit down and fold his hands in his lap, holding his soul in patience for eternity? In truth, his plight is, as expressed in passionate outburst by an ardent Sâdhaka, "My mind understands, but the heart will not; it is a case of the dwarf trying to catch the moon!" The word "impossible" does not exist for the aspirant. He knows that God makes even the

impossible possible, that He can, if He wills, pass a camel through the eye of a needle.

* * * *

130. The spirit of a true devotee—of a true Sâdhaka—is: "I find delight in practising Japa and meditation and cannot help doing these. I practise them because there is no other way to soothe the heart. I practise because Japa and meditation are the very breath of my life, without them it is not possible for me to live. God is the Life of my life, the Self of my self. He must be realised somehow. If I do not find Him I shall go mad and die, and this life itself will be in vain!" If there be such intense yearning, such madness of love, such unshaken tenacity of purpose, He is sure to bestow His favour on the devotee, for He is all-merciful. Without fail, He will show Himself, if one calls on Him with all sincerity and earnestness, if one renounces everything for His sake and takes refuge in Him alone.

* * *

131. But does that yearning, that feeling that He is the sole refuge, come easily?

It comes only in the last birth of one who has strenuously devoted himself to spiritual practices for the attainment of the Goal in many previous lives. This rare trait shone with undiminished brilliance all through the life of Nâg Mahâsaya, the great householder disciple of Sri Ramakrishna. What an amazing state of God-intoxication filled his whole being all the time! What whole-souled absorption without any awareness of the body! What wonderful humility, holding himself as the lowliest of God's creatures! What intense longing for God-vision burned in his soul and consumed his earthly frame! He who has not seen him can form no idea of his unique personality. Wonderful life! Wonderful example!

* * *

132. God cannot be seen unless the mind becomes tranquil, pure and stainless. Unless the water of a lake remains calm and transparent, it does not reflect anything at all, or does so only indistinctly. If the mirror is covered with dust, it does not reflect an image or else makes it look blurred. For this reason repeated practice

and renunciation are the only means or discipline for the purification of the mind. Even that which is felt to be difficult or impossible becomes easy of attainment by dint of constant practice. Whatever is regularly practised, gradually becomes part of one's very nature. Along with this, the spirit of renunciation must be cultivated. "All is transient and insubstantial, God alone is real and eternal." If, grasping this, one can fully surrender one's whole heart and soul to Him alone, pure love will arise in the heart. If that comes, what else remains to seek after and to possess? "The Lord is of the nature of ineffable Love." When that love, which is beyond speech or mind, deepens and abides in the heart, then it reveals itself as changed into the form of the Beloved One who is Love embodied.

*　　　*　　　*

133. Whatever be your income, try to save a little out of it every month. The Master used to say that it is very necessary for the householder to save. It becomes very useful in the future, because health, service, business, wealth, kith and kin—

nothing whatever is permanent. If in youth
or in middle age, a person deluded by
the enjoyment of sense pleasures, under
the influence of bad company and evil
tendencies and habits, spends without a
thought for the future, as much as he
earns or more, then he is sure to come
to endless grief. Diseases and ailments,
dangers and calamities, cares and anxieties,
are always present in the world. In old
age one is a prey to disease and decrepitude,
and loses with rapid strides the capacity
to work. If there be some saving, then
one does not succumb to difficulties, nor
has he to moan and lament, but can spend
the rest of his life independently and with
peace of mind, thinking of God and the
Spirit.

*   *   *

134. "Whatever be the situation, O
Mother, in which Thou placest me—that is
verily a blessing to me if I do not forget
Thee!"—this sang a Sâdhaka. He, the Lord,
is All-Good, the Inner-Guide of all. He
knows what is good for one, and what is
good for another, and so dispenses things
in such a way that they may be good for

you as well as good for each and all, for
He has to look after the whole universe.
One ought to know that surely He cannot
do good to one alone, at the cost of injury
to all the rest. By always thinking of
"me and mine", and confining ourselves
within a narrow circle, we desire happiness
only for ourselves and for our kith and
kin, and try to have it at any cost, without
caring if it will produce evil to others.
There is no unadulterated happiness, minus
pain, in the world. Both are so mixed up
together that if you want one, the other
will come of itself. So we only bungle by
wanting to have what we like. The Lord
knows infinitely better than we do what
will be for our real good, because He is
All-knowing. Misery and happiness cannot
disturb the equanimity of the mind of one
who, being content with whatever He dis-
poses, takes refuge in Him alone and lives
in the world putting full reliance upon
Him.

*　　　*　　　*

135. "Various kinds of obstructions
spring up without warning for him whose
mind is attached to worldly objects, even

if he retires to the forest. But if a person is engaged in good work and restrains the five senses, even though he lives at home, that itself is Tapasyâ (practising austerity). The home of a man without attachment is itself the Tapovana (hermitage)."—thus says the *Hitopadesha*. Wherever you may go, or whatever you may do, with the mind uncontrolled, you will inevitably have to suffer, and there will be no escape. Besides, you will also be entangled in varieties of newer and unthought-of bondages. But for one who can bring his mind under control by spiritual practices, who is free from attachment to objects though living in the world, home or forest is just the same. Wherever he may live, whatever he may do, he is ever-free and full of bliss.

*　　　*　　　*

136. The average man cannot remain even a moment without talking. If he does not have anyone to talk to, he is sure to converse mentally. What else is thinking? It is talking to oneself. If that is so, is it not far preferable to take the name of God and to think of Him as much as you can, instead of fruitlessly

engaging in foolish or futile talk? Of course it is unavoidable for the sake of work or business to engage in various kinds of talk with people. But when you are alone, or have not any important work on hand, it is surely desirable to make the habit of remembering God and taking His name, instead of entertaining other thoughts which are of little value. It is necessary to practise Japa at all times to ward off other thoughts; for Japa means continuous uninterrupted repetition of the name of God.

* * *

137. While doing Japa, one should think of Him alone, regarding the name and the object signified by the name as identical. The name is identical with the one named, that is to say, as soon as you utter a name, it is understood to mean the person whose name it is. If you call somebody by name, his image simultaneously floats before the mind, and he also responds to the call or comes near. Japa is exactly that, if it is properly done and if the mind be fixed on Him alone. But there must be this much faith—that the call will reach Him

and that He will respond. It is also the case with prayer, if it is sincere and ardent. By repeated practice of Japa, this feeling of certainty and nearness is firmly established and the mind becomes absorbed in Him, and His Presence is unmistakably felt. So the scriptures say, "Realisation comes through Japa".

*   *   *

138. Yogis say that there are seven lotuses (Chakras) or nerve centres in the human body. There·is at the base the four-petalled lotus *Mulâdhâra* in the rectal region, the six-petalled *Swâdhisthâna* at the root of the genital organ, the ten-petalled *Manipura* at the back of the navel, the twelve-petalled *Anâhata* in the heart, the sixteen-petalled *Vishuddha* at the back of the throat, the two-petalled *Ajnâ* between the eye-brows, and the thousand-petalled lotus called *Sahasrâra* at the top of the head. Besides, there are the three nerves, namely, the *Idâ*, the *Pingalâ* and the *Sushumnâ*, to the left, to the right and in the middle respectively of the spinal column, going up through it. The nerve-current, *Sushumnâ*, ends in the

Sahasrâra, the seat of Brahman, after passing right through the centre of the six lotuses, one after another. But the passage of the *Sushumnâ* remains closed until the *Kulakundalini*, the coiled-up serpent-like power, awakens. The *Kulakundalini* is the power of Knowledge of the Self, is of the essence of Intelligence and Brahman. This Shakti is dormant—inactive and unperceived —asleep, as it were, lying coiled up like a sleeping serpent in the *Mulâdhâra* lotus in all human beings, and is awakened by Yoga, meditation, spiritual practices, etc. When that power in the *Mulâdhâra* awakens and unites with the Supreme Shiva, or Paramâtman (Supreme Self) in the *Sahasrâra*, after rising along the channel of the *Sushumnâ* nerve, piercing and passing successively through the *Mulâdhâra*, the *Swâdhisthâna*, the *Manipura*, the *Anâhata*, the *Vishuddha* and the *Ajnâ* centres, then the nectar of a supersensuous sweetness flows from the union of the two, drinking which the individual is merged in *Samâdhi*. Only then does the individual awaken to the Knowledge of the Supreme Self and attain Perfection.

Moreover, various wonderful spiritual experiences, like the perception of all-encompassing self-luminous light or the glorious vision of the Chosen Ideal, occur. Sometimes, this Kundalini-Shakti awakens of itself, or with little effort, by the grace of the Guru and the Supreme Lord, due to the force of Sâdhanâs and good works done by the aspirant in past lives. The Master used to say that the body does not usually last more than twenty-one days in that state of Nirvikalpa Samâdhi (the state of Pure Consciousness beyond all mental modifications), when the individual is merged in the Supreme Self, or Brahman, —becomes one with It. This, in short, is what is known as *Shat-chakra-bheda*, or the piercing of the six Chakras, or mystic nerve-centres.

* * *

139. But those who are world-teachers, *Achâryakotis* (specially gifted spiritual teachers) or *Iswarakotis* (persons with Divine authority), who are born in the human body for the good of the world or for the sake of fulfilling a special divine mission, can and do bring the awakened

9

serpent-power down again along that passage from the *Sahasrâra* (head) to the *Anâhata* (heart) and remain in a special state of divine mood, called Bhâvamukha, rejecting for themselves even the Bliss of Brahman. They alternately dwell in the states of absolute and relative consciousness, that is to say, they sometimes lose themselves in Samâdhi or God-consciousness and bring themselves down to the human plane, with the sole purpose of delivering, out of compassion, thousands of souls from the delusion and bondage of nescience.

*   *   *

140. Swamiji (Swami Vivekananda) has said that only very rarely does the power of Kundalini of some great soul awaken of itself, without his having properly followed the usual scientific methods of Yoga as laid down in the Hindu Scriptures. It is like the sudden discovery of some unexpected truth. Suppose that, while walking along a road, a man stumbles and finds something shining underneath the stone that has been displaced by chance. Lifting the stone, he discovers underneath jars up-

on jars filled with gold coins. It is like that.
But those who suddenly realise some higher
truth in this manner, may well cause as
much mischief to the world as good, by
their fanaticism and narrowness of outlook.
At the time of congregational singing of
religious songs many weep and wail and
dance wildly till they lose consciousness
due to an exuberance of emotion suddenly
excited. A portion of their Kundalini
power has, no doubt, somewhat awakened
for a little while, but this often has a
terrible reaction. It is generally found that
the desire to indulge in their vicious habits,
or their craving for name and fame by posing themselves as great devotees or spiritual
adepts before the public, grows very strong,
and they finally degenerate into hypocrites
and charlatans.

* * *

141. As men see the sun with the help
of sunlight itself, and not by striking a
light, so God is seen through His own
grace only, and not through the limited
powers of men. But the sun cannot be'
seen if clouds come and cover it. Similarly,
Avidyâ (nescience), or Mâyâ, shuts out

the vision of God. The winds of prayer and spiritual discipline blow away those clouds, and He reveals Himself. Prayer and spiritual discipline are not the causes to bring about the revelation of God, for He is self-revealing; they only take away the covering and the obstructions.

* * *

142. Jnâna, Bhakti, Purity, Renunciation, Yearning for God—these are Divine qualities, His own essential characteristics. With these He endows in advance the person to whom He wants to show favour or reveal Himself. When these virtues are found in a person, it is clear that the dark night of delusion is about to pass away and the glorious dawn will break before long. Do you know the following saying of the Master? A Zamindar (landlord) importuned by his tenant, not only agreed to visit his house and partake of his hospitality but also sent certain necessaries to the tenant's house, because he knew that the tenant was poor and would not be able to procure those costly things. God shows favour only to one who longs for Him with a yearning heart, having

renounced everything for His sake.

*   *   *

143. Does God, then have likes and dis-
likes, favour some and deny others? Does
He show no favour to, or is He dissatisfied
with, one who lives in the world forgetful
of Him, engrossed in wife, children, family
and property? How can that be? All,
whether devotees or revilers, whether sannyasins or householders, are, verily, His
children. The mother has the same love
and affection for the child, even when it is
absorbed in play and forgetful of her, as
she has when it cries for her, throwing
away its playthings, and she drops her
work and takes it in her lap and caresses
it. The mother thinks that as long as the
child is lost in play, it is quite happy, so
why disturb it? Let it go on playing!
When it no longer finds the game interest-
ing, it leaves it, or disbands the playthings,
then it wants her alone, and is comforted
by nothing else—then it is that the mother
comes and takes it in her lap. In truth,
can there be ever any play that gives that
happiness which the child feels sucking
the breast in its mother's arms? But all

the same, it does not give up playing! This is called Mâyâ.

* * *

144. However much it may thunder or storms blow and rains pour, however the lightning flashes and the thunderbolt strikes, still the Châtak bird, without being in the least frightened, turns its gaze skyward and slakes its thirst by drinking rain-water to its heart's content. It never drinks, as the tradition holds, the water of the tank on the ground below, even if it be dying of thirst. Similarly, one who is a sincere devotee of God, looks to Him alone to quench the burning thirst of his soul and has no expectation of anything from anybody except God. He knows that everything whatsoever that happens, is a gift of His mercy. He is never perturbed, however much he may see His terrifying face, and no matter whether pain and misery, want and poverty, calamities and other evils befall him in the world, he sees in them only the face of his Beloved. He knows that God is Good, that whatever He does, He does for his good and for the good of all. To be discontented means,

finding fault with Him, and complaining
against Him and His Dispensation. The
true devotee cannot do that even for the
very life of him.

* * *

145. He is the Guru who takes God-
ward and along the path to peace the
Jiva, burned by the fire of threefold
misery of life (pain—bodily, mental and
those due to natural causes). The relation
between the Guru and the disciple is
that of a spiritual father and a son or a
daughter. The worldly father begets a
son. The Guru delivers the disciple from
birth and death by showing him the
Supreme Truth. The paternal debt can
be repaid by continuing the family line
by performing the Srâddha ceremonies
(sacramental ceremonies done by a son
after his father's death for his welfare
hereafter). But the debt to the Guru cannot be repaid even by offering one's all,
for he delivers the disciple from Avidyâ
(nescience). As one or another virtue of
ancestors is inherited by sons and grand-
sons in varying degrees, so also is some
spirituality certain to descend to the dis-

ciples and to the disciples of their disciples
in the line of Gurus.

* * *

146. The Reality cannot be attained if
one is impatient. The Supreme Self alone
is the only Reality, Essence, and Truth;
and everything else—the manifested universe—is unreal, non-essence and deceptive,
and therefore fit only to be rejected. Great
patience and perseverance are needed for
the knowledge of this fact to become
established.

* * *

147. The real "YOU" will truly exist
only when the little "you", or ego, will
cease to exist. Your true life will begin
when the little "you" has died. "Vexations
vanish when 'I' (small ego) dies."

* * *

148. Thinking that our life and death
depend upon this world, it is we ourselves
who create all manner of troubles and
turmoils for ourselves in an attempt to
safeguard "our own rights and interests".
We feel unhappy ourselves and have no
scruple also in causing loss or ruin to
others. Day and night we exhaust our-

selves by running about to gain our ends, fighting for life, and flying at one another's throats. As people say, "O, I have not the time even to die!" Such is the Mâyâ (illusive spell) of Mahâmâyâ, the Divine Mother, the great Conjuror of Cosmic Illusion! The Mother sits and watches the play and smiles. It is like kittens or puppies at play, getting into a scrap and inflicting sharp nips upon one another now and then. We attach undue gravity to the play and get ourselves so much mixed up and involved in it, that we become utterly heedless of consequences and care not even if we die in the fray. The play no doubt becomes very absorbing, just as a drama seems real if the actors and actresses identify themselves fully with their parts. But that is only for the time being—a temporary phase.

*   *   *

149. This play comes to an end only when the awareness comes that the world itself, that this life of ours is all merely a play. When we have an evil dream we sometimes laugh or weep like a madman; sometimes we find ourselves helplessly

carried away in a sea of deadly perils, and groan in fear or cry out in agony. It seems there is no end of horrors. Reason and judgement depart and even the queerest things appear to be quite natural and true. But the dream breaks as soon as we wake up and realise that it is, after all, a dream. Returning to the normal state we think, "Ah, what a relief!" Or we may dream a pleasant dream—for instance, that we have won two lacs of rupees in a lottery, and are beside ourselves with joy; and when the dream breaks suddenly, we give ourselves up to depression. Our whole life is nothing else but a long-drawn, continuous dream like that. It is a texture of good and bad dreams, of hope and despair, of pleasure and pain, as its warp and woof. As long as this dream lasts, we regard everything as real. The universe melts away into nothingness when the dream breaks. What remains then?—The Ever-True exists and reveals Its own Self by Its own nature.

*   *   *

150. Why should God be angry with anybody? Anger is caused when some-

thing stands in the way of a keenly desired objective. Is there anything which He desires, or which He has yet to obtain, or which He cannot obtain? And who is there to put obstacles in His way? He expects nothing from us. It does not matter the least to Him whether we call on Him or remain forgetful of Him. The gain or loss, pleasure or pain, good or bad, appertains to ourselves alone.

*   *   *

151. The Upanishads declare that one who knows that he knows Brahman knows It not. But one who knows that Brahman is beyond the reach of speech and mind and is of the nature of Knowledge Absolute, and therefore beyond all limited knowledge and experience, knows It truly. Then he becomes Brahman Itself. Who can know the Knower? By being known, the Knower becomes an object of knowledge, and therefore limited. Whatever is limited and is within the realm of space, time and causation, has birth and destruction, merits and defects, and hence can never give Mukti, or Perfection. So what would be the good of knowing or worshipping

or attaining such a limited object?

*　　　　*　　　　*

152. Brahman is of the nature of Truth, Knowledge, Bliss and Infinity. These are not Its attributes but Its nature or essence. Attributes do limit. They are not eternal because they grow and decay. Brahman is, therefore, beyond all attributes or predicates, beyond everything. One can only say of It that It is "Not this, not this". Even that, also, cannot be said when Its full nature is realised, because the sense of duality vanishes altogether at that stage. Who is there, then, to say or express anything of it? But in Its aspect with Form, as Personal God, Brahman is the possessor of infinite, blessed qualities.

*　　　　*　　　　*

153. If Brahman be "One without a second", wherefrom, and why, did Mâyâ come and act upon It? This is an old, old question, leading to no end, since no answer can ever be given from within the realm of Mâyâ. And who is there to ask this question after one goes beyond Mâyâ? For nothing called Mâyâ then

exists for such a one. In that state, both
the seer and the seen are destroyed, and the
idea of oneness alone remains. One then
has the intuitive perception that Brahman
alone exists, ever the same in the past,
present and future, shining in Its tran-
scendent Glory—that Mâyâ has never
touched It, that the sense of duality is
mere illusion, and that, "I am Brahman,
the Absolute".

* * *

154. He alone is a disciple who strives
heart and soul to follow in letter and in
spirit the instructions of the Guru with
sincere regard for and faith in them, and
who devotes himself to his Guru's service
for the Guru's pleasure and satisfaction
only. Do not regard the Guru as a mere
man. If the disciple looks upon him as the
visible God, and loves and worships him
with all his heart, he makes speedy progress in the spiritual path and attains the
Cherished Goal. It is the qualified Guru
who brings about the union with the
Supreme Guru (the Lord as the Chosen
Ideal) dwelling in the heart. It is through
the Guru alone that the spiritual current

is transmitted to the disciple. Whatever
is desired can be won through the grace of
the Guru. But the disciple must also have
the requisite qualifications to deserve it.
Purity of body, mind and speech, intense
longing for Jnâna, Bhakti, Mukti, aversion
to worldly objects, and indomitable perseverance, are required. The Guru, too, must
be one who is conversant with the true
import of the Shâstras, sinless and established in Brahman. He must be one who
is without desire for worldly enjoyment,
selfless and devoted to doing good to
others. His love and compassion should be
the same for all beings.

*   *   *

155. A father and the Guru desire
defeat from the son and the disciple respectively; that is to say, they sincerely wish,
"May my son, my disciple, surpass me in
greatness. May he be more eminent and
win more honour and respect than I."
But a father entertains expectations of
many things from his son in the future,
while the Guru expects nothing for himself from the disciple. His nature is to
give, and he gives without thought of

return. Swamiji used to say to us, "Let me see each one of you greater than Vivekananda! I shall be very glad and happy then, and shall regard my coming as worth while."

* * *

156. A corpse struck with a sabre feels nothing. If the body can be made into a corpse, that is to say, if self-identification with the body can be destroyed, then however severe may be the blows that fall on one in life, they will never be felt! Only men of this nature do not react to circumstances, like ordinary mortals, and are free while living in the body. To them both the home and the cremation-ground—life and death—are the same.

* * *

157. Attachment to this body—self-identification with the body—is verily the root of all evil. All fears, errors and vices originate from it. There is no sin a man shrinks from committing—theft, swindling, ruining people, and even murder—in order to preserve his body and live. "Woman and gold" becomes the only deity he worships. As a result, he em-

braces pain in expectation of pleasure, and hugs death itself in the hope of saving his blessed body. He fears death at every moment. But the enlightened soul, who has been able to rise above the body-sense, is ready to sacrifice his life cheerfully for even a lowly animal. This body is nothing to him—an utterly insignificant thing. Men are of two classes—brute-men and god-men—those who identify themselves with the body, and those without body-sense. The individual in the bondage of the body is the brute-man, while the other, without the sense of the body, is the god-man.

*   *   *

158. The fruits of all actions—good, bad or indifferent—should be dedicated to God. It is not the right attitude to feel proud of our good actions and works of religious merit (Punya), and keep their fruits to ourselves for our own enjoyment, thinking that it is *we* who have done them, while we dedicate to Him the fruits of our bad and sinful deeds, knowing that they will cause us suffering. By doing so, we simply try to shift our responsibility to

Him, thinking that the bad actions are due to His will, that we have acted as He made us act, and thus escape the dire nemesis! It is mere practising self-deception. God gives everything to him who dedicates his all to Him without retaining anything, and without a thought for his own self.

*   *   *

159. That holy name, or sound, which delivers the mind from Avidyâ (nescience) is called the Mantra.

*   *   *

160. Avidyâ has been defined in the following way in the philosophical system of Patanjali: Avidyâ is the sense of permanence in things impermanent (the mundane world), the sense of purity in things impure (the body, etc.), the sense of pleasure in pain (that is, in the enjoyment of worldly objects, which ultimately cause pain), the sense of self-hood in non-self (identification of wife, children, etc., with oneself, as from the point of ultimate Reality, they are not one's own). Avidyâ is without beginning, as its starting-point, or cause, cannot be ascertained; and there

is also no cessation or end of it with reference to the phenomenal process of the universe. It exists in seed form even at the time of *Pralaya,* or the dissolution of the whole universe at the end of each *Kalpa,* or cycle, and it remains in the unmanifested state, till it emerges again at the time of creation, or, better, projection. As long as the knowledge of Reality is not attained, men are subject to birth and death again and again and suffer various kinds of miseries, having to be reborn either as men, animals or birds, etc. according to their nature and Karma.

*   *   *

161. Is it then in vain to try for Mukti? Certainly, no! Because Avidyâ has an end for particular individuals. When, after endless suffering, discrimination and renunciation (Viveka and Vairâgya) arise, and the Jiva takes refuge in God, then Avidyâ is destroyed, root and branch, and knowledge comes, through the grace of the Lord. So has the infinitely merciful Lord repeatedly declared in the Gita: "Having come to this fleeting world, full of pain, worship and take refuge in Me

alone. I shall deliver you from all sins, and take you to the realm of Bliss across the sea of the world of existence, characterised by birth and death, and so difficult to cross."

* * *

162. There is a Bengali saying: "Bring the food to my mouth; it is too much for me to move! Bless your fathers and their meritorious acts!" Nowadays, most people belong to that category. Nobody wants to exert himself; everybody wants to gain his ends gratuitously, or by some crafty trick. Especially in regard to things spiritual, people seek to avoid all effort and toil, which they dislike, and to have everything done for them by others. After sitting with closed eyes an hour or so for a few days or a few months, they grumble and complain, "Alas! I am achieving nothing; I can't collect my mind; I don't feel I am making any progress," and so on. Swamiji used to say, "Is God a vegetable, a bunch of spinach, or a fish, that you throw down a few coins and buy Him?" Why be so impatient for immediate results? Go on striving, and your effort will bear fruit of itself in the fulness of time. Men

of the world pay wages if you work for them; and will not God do so if you work for Him? Faith, steadfastness, sincere love, patience and perseverance are needed. Does a seed sprout up into a tree and bear fruit as soon as it is planted? One has to bestow so much toil and attention and continue to do this for a long while, before one can reap the fruits in due season.

* * *

163. It is seen that many people practise Japa and meditation with great earnestness for some weeks after taking initiation, and derive considerable joy and benefit from it. After that, this earnestness suddenly melts away, and they are not at all inclined even to sit down for meditation any more. They feel their hearts empty, as it were, and find themselves helpless and without any support to hold on to. However, there is nothing to be afraid of or to grow despondent about. Everything has its ups and downs, ebb and flow, union and separation. In the life of the aspirant, likewise, there is hope and despair, light and darkness. If this happens to one whose heart burns passionately to realise God or to gain

spirituality, then his yearning is further intensified; he has no rest, but cries out in the agony of his heart, imploring Divine favour. Then, by the Lord's grace, he again devotes himself to meditation with redoubled enthusiasm, and makes more rapid and greater progress, and finds greater joy than ever before.

* * *

164. There is another class of people whose "new love" or upsurge of first devotion cools down gradually: the mind loses its early vigour and ardour, and spiritual practices finally become a travesty of their former nature. Year after year practices are continued as a dull round of irksome daily duties, as a kind of forced labour, or as a mere formal observance of the letter of the Law. Or the practices are dropped altogether, and deceptive excuses are trotted forth, on the score of various worldly duties and obligations, want of time, physical unfitness and what not. In cases like this it is obvious, that these people took initiation or renounced the world in a fit of temporary exuberance of emotion; or during a momentary spiritual

mood or feeling of Vairâgya or dispassion, caused by some severe blow or bereavement in the world; or in the hope of gaining some particular selfish end. Not much of spirituality can be expected of them.

*   *   *

165. Many people think, "When the Guru has initiated me, he has taken the responsibility for all my sins; there is nothing more for me to do or to worry about; everything will be achieved through his grace alone!" To shift the responsibility for sin to another, or to take the burden of another's sin on one's own shoulders, is not so easy as is generally believed. If that were so, the world would have been a different place to live in, as everybody could have become sinless without effort! If you wish to give your burden of sin to the Guru or to God, you have also to give away the share of your Punya, or meritorious acts, at the same time. But if you merely want to give that portion of your actions which are to bring you pain or suffering, while keeping for yourself the share of your good actions which will bring you enjoyment or pleasure in this life or the

next—then neither do you give nor does He truly accept the sin. Then again, if any one becomes sinless, after having thus transferred his burden of sin, he can surely no longer engage himself in any sinful activity. So if sin or evil tendencies still remain in the mind even after initiation, and if a new life is not gained thereby, it is obvious that the sins behaved at the time of initiation exactly as they are supposed to do at the time of bathing in the Gangâ which washes away all sin, as Sri Ramakrishna used to remark in a joking mood: "The sins sit crouching in the branches of a nearby tree on the bank of the Gangâ at the time of bathing, but no sooner does the bather come out of the river than they swoop back again on to his shoulders."

*　　　*　　　*

166. Jesting apart, just think, if you have even only a grain of faith, love, or devotion for your Guru, could your heart ever bear the thought of making him suffer pain and torment by placing all your evils and sins on his shoulders? Is he a scavenger's cart? Only those who are without that

feeling of love and who are intensely selfish and attached to worldly objects can become so ignoble. They are, in truth, not fit even to be counted as disciples. But those who have firm faith in and love for the Guru cannot commit sin any more, lest the Guru might have to suffer for it. Aye, it is of such disciples that he takes the burden of sin. In truth, God in the form of the Guru takes this burden upon himself, and absolves the disciple of sin.

* * *

167. Nevertheless it is true that some of the disciples' sins are visited upon the Guru. For it is often seen that, if many are given Mantra-Dikshâ (initiation) without discrimination and scrutiny about their moral nature and fitness, some mortal illness takes possession of the physical frame of the pure, sinless Guru and shortens his life. But urged by the impetus of doing good to others and of leading them Godward, the selfless, eminent Guru of boundless mercy, despite full knowledge of this, takes no thought for his own body and lays down his life by inches for the welfare of the

disciples. Incarnations of God take upon themselves the burden of others' sins, and so they too have to suffer from various diseases on that score. Sri Ramakrishna used to say, "This disease (cancer in the throat) with which my body is afflicted is due to my taking upon me the sins of Girish."— (His great dramatist disciple).

*   *   *

168. What to speak of the body, which is a mere trifle, the worthy Guru gives away to the disciple without stint, scruple or any thought of return, the whole of his invaluable spiritual treasure, accumulated through lifelong austerities and spiritual discipline. If the disciple be pure in spirit and an ardent devotee of God, then only can he feel and fully realise in his heart the force of the spiritual current transmitted by the Guru. The more a disciple advances with firm faith and conviction along the path of spiritual practice pointed out by the Guru, the purer his mind becomes and the more he comprehends the greatness of the Guru's power as well as his grace. Realisation is attained by a combination of the grace of the Guru and the

untiring efforts of the disciple.

*   *   *

169. Never forget that the aim and end of human life is Realisation of God. If you wear out your life in eating, sleeping and sense pleasure, like an animal, and in idle talk, gossip and fruitless activity, your life will pass in vain and you will only reap misery. Apply yourself with all your energy, with all your heart and soul, for realising God, as long as you have strength and vigour left in your body and mind. Never for any reason slacken in your efforts. "These practices can be done later on, these will be possible only when God wills it so, or is propitious"—these are the words of do-nothing sluggards, those who never sincerely intend to do anything. Nothing good will ever be achieved by them.

*   *   *

170. The best time of life is from the sixteenth to the thirtieth year, when the body retains the fullest capacity for work, and when the qualities which are helpful for achieving the desired end, such as enthusiasm, initiative, courage, self-confi-

dence, strength of will and firmness of
resolution, are of themselves present in
the mind. Do you bank on the idea that
you will devote your mind to spiritual
Sâdhanâs in old age after having squan-
dered away this invaluable period of life?
Vain hope! This is mere self-deception.
Even if the mind or the spirit be willing
then, you will find that the body or the
flesh will be failing, unable to bear the
strain. It will then be a constant prey to
all kinds of chronic diseases, will be dis-
tracted with sickness and pain, will feel
exhausted and prostrate by a little exertion
and get indolent and drowsy. Helpless,
with high hopes and ambitions frustrated,
thoroughly dependent on others for the
least service or favour, life will be unbearable. Granting even that the body be fairly
strong, still all the Samskâras or resultant
tendencies of your past life and your life-
long habits and preoccupations, as also
your inordinate attachment to wife, children and grandchildren, etc., will have you
bound so firmly that neither will the mind
turn easily to the thought of God or
make a sincere effort to devote itself to

spiritual practices for realising Him, nor
will you be able, howsoever you may try,
to deflect the mind from its worldly rut.
Apart from all that, life is uncertain and
may end today or tomorrow. Who can
say that he will live to old age, and will
then find enough time and leisure? Whatever you have to do, do it now; for if you
put it off till "tomorrow", that tomorrow
may never come.

*   *   *

171. It is most essential for a Sâdhaka to
practise the following virtues and rules:

(1) Firm belief in God and reliance on
Him. (2) Observance of Brahmacharya, or
restraint of the senses, which means renunciation of lustful desire. By pondering over
the insubstantial and evil nature of sense-
objects, you should give up your attachment to and thirst for them, and should
be free of all passion. The fullest development of body, mind and intelligence
is impossible without control of the sexual
instinct. If this is observed without break
for twelve years, a fine nerve called Medhâ,
the nerve of retentive faculty and intuition,

is developed, which characterises a sage or a magnetic personality. From this arises the capacity for grasping and retaining subtle truths. Then one comes to enjoy perfect health, the body and the face shine with a divine lustre, and an irrepressible vigour comes to the mind. Power of work and intellectual acumen will increase manifold. (3) Moderation and regularity in food and recreation. Food should be non-exciting, nourishing and easily digestible. Gluttony has to be avoided. The purpose of eating is not to tickle the palate, but to keep the body healthy and fit for work. Breathing fresh air and some light exercises are beneficial. No work of any kind—not to mention any great work—can be done by sick, invalid, weak, sleepy, lazy or wanton persons. (4) Bad company, evil discourses, carping criticism of others behind their backs, and wasting time in meaningless activities should be shunned. Seek holy company, study the scriptures, think good thoughts and discriminate between the real and the unreal. (5) Always keep your eye on the aim and ideal of life, and exert your body, mind

and soul for realising that. Go on with
your spiritual practices with infinite patience
and perseverance. Never allow despair
or lassitude to assail your mind. If you
worship God with all your heart and soul,
knowing Him to be the one Beloved and
your all-in-all, without caring anything for
your personal happiness and comfort and
for the fruits of your Karma, you will
enjoy supreme peace and bliss.

                    *   *   *

172. The whole life of an aspirant
after Truth is one of continuous spiritual
endeavour—and not of doing Japa and
meditation for an hour or two at the ap-
pointed time and remaining absorbed in
sordid worldly pursuits for the rest of
the day and night. That never builds
up spiritual life. Only when spirituality
blossoms forth in every thought, action and
circumstance of life, when it is in the very
marrow of one's being, as it were, then
only can one be called truly spiritual.
Work with your hands, talk to different
people about work and business with your
mouth, but keep the mind fixed on God,
and know that this alone—this living in

God—is the one thing for which one comes into this world, the one thing that makes life worth-while. Humility, selflessness, non-attachment and the knowledge that God is the only Reality or Truth are the means of abiding in that state. It is difficult, no doubt, but it comes by long and repeated practice. Sri Ramakrishna used to illustrate this by his parable of the village woman flattening rice and at the same time suckling her baby, calculating old dues or settling accounts or barganing prices with customers, though all the while her mind is really on the pestle, lest it should come down on her hand.

*   *   *

173. In the early stages Japa and meditation should be practised according to a routine. The mind is by nature averse to work and exertion, and very often seeks excuses to avoid and shirk them. It will run about in other directions instead of doing the task to which you set it. If you do not keep it engaged in any task, it will lead you into all manner of worthless and mischievous things. So it is rightly said, the idle mind is the Devil's workshop.

In order to bring it under control it must be forcibly bound by a set of hard and fast rules. After proper deliberation, draw up such a daily routine as will be practicable for you to observe. And resolve firmly that, whatever be the situation in which you may find yourself, or whatever other work may turn up, you will never fail to observe the routine you have framed. Such steadfastness and determination are essential to spiritual progress. Meals, recreation, study, exercise, sleep, work, meditation and spiritual practices, and even amusement and fun, sports and play—indeed, all kinds of healthy activity—should have their fixed time. If you spend your days in a desultory fashion, life will be wasted. After drawing up a routine you should admonish the mind severely, saying to it, "Look here, Sir, whether you like it or not, you will have to observe these rules!" For some time the mind will prove obdurate and unmanageable, will resist all your attempts to induce it to work, and will run away in different directions. You should, however, never give up the effort to bring it back forcibly and put it to work, coaxing it at the same time. Moreover, keep watch to see that the work is being properly done. Taming the mind is like the taming of a wild animal. It requires infinite patience, perseverance and will-power. When the mind at last discovers that there is no way of escape, it will cease playing monkey tricks, and being obedient will quietly do your bidding. This is called Abhyâsa-yoga, the path of repeated practice. Know that there is no other way than this to bring the mind under control.

*   *   *

174. If you can follow this Yoga of practice continuously for three or four years, even like swallowing medicine, however hard, dry, insipid or nasty it may taste, you will then find how sweet and life-giving, like unto nectar, and how full of the purest bliss, is this practising of meditation and spiritual discipline! What dreadful toil students have to undergo, keeping awake till midnight, thoughtlessly sacrificing the body and ruining the health, to get through one or other of the college examinations! On the top of it all, there is constant fear, anxiety and worry. It is

11

like passing through a crisis—as if life
and death hang on getting through the
examination successfully! And to what end
is all this? Is it not for the uncertain
prospect of securing a big job, earning
money or getting name and fame and so
forth, with a view to living in comfort and
happiness? The struggle for the realisation
of God is certainly easier than this, at
least in the sense that it need not be
fraught with such fear and anxiety about
the ultimate result, as that is fully assured.
If one applies oneself assiduously and
strenuously for realising God by giving up
all other work and taking the inexorable
vow, "Either the fulfilment of the aim or
the destruction of the body", then the
Lord will, without the shadow of a doubt,
reveal Himself and confer such invaluable treasures on the devotee that all the
riches, fortune and pleasures of the world
will grow insignificant in comparison.
Having crossed death, he becomes heir to
Immortality.

*   *   *

175. Mahârâj (Swâmi Brahmânanda)
used to say: "When a disciple of mine

comes to me shortly after initiation and says, 'Why, Sir, I have been practising Japa and meditation all these days, but I am achieving nothing at all. I cannot control my mind at all, and I am not getting any peace or joy,' I give no reply at the time, as if his words have not reached my ears. Two or three years after that he himself says, 'It appears now that I am making some progress after such a long time. I am having some joy and peace.'" So I say to you: Go on practising hard the spiritual disciplines and prayers with all your heart continuously for two or three years, and then you will experience joy. You want to be men of Realisation for the mere asking, by some trick, without doing anything yourself! Is it not sheer madness?

*　　*　　*

176. Even Sri Sârada Devi (the Holy Mother) used to be pestered by the insensate importunities of her children (disciples). She would say, "How fine were the various devotees of Sri Ramakrishna's time! Those who come now only say, 'Mother, show us the Lord!' 'Show the Master to us!' 'Why don't we have His

vision?' 'You can surely do this for us, if you will!' How many of our venerable Yogis and Rishis of old failed to find Him even after practising severe austerities for ages upon ages! And yet these expect to achieve everything in a trice! They neither carry out spiritual discipline, nor practise austerities or self-control, and yet they say, 'Show Him to us at once!' Who knows what evil deeds they have committed in so many past lives! How can they hope for higher things before these have been gradually worked out? If Realisation is not had in this birth, it may come in the next, or it may even come in the life after the next. But come it must if you go on working for it. Is realisation of God so easy? Only, this time, with the advent of Thâkur (Sri Ramakrishna) and the path shown by him, it is easier, that is all. They are living a worldly life and begetting children every year, and yet they come and say, Why don't I have the vision of the Divine Master? Women used to go to Thâkur and say, 'Why does not the mind turn to God? Why doesn't it get steady?' and

so on. The Master would answer them:
'Ah! How can that be now? There is
still the smell of child-birth about you.
Let that first leave you. It will come in
the fulness of time. It is enough for this
life that you have come to me. In the next
life the spiritual path will be easy of
attainment for you.' A vision may be had
of Him in dreams, perhaps. But actually
seeing Him with these eyes, or His showing Himself to a devotee by assuming a
body—to how many does that happen?
That is rare good fortune, indeed."

*   *   *

177. Sri Ramakrishna used to say, "I
have done sixteen annas;* it will be enough
if you do only one anna." It is, in truth,
beyond the powers of a mortal to do a
hundredth part of the rigours of the superhuman austerities for God-realisation that
Sri Ramakrishna underwent. It is however
necessary to do at least that one anna as
asked by him. But it is only when one
attempts to do the full measure of the
sixteen parts that one may possibly
succeed in doing one part only. If you

* A rupee, that is, full measure of Sâdhanâ.

proceed one step towards God, He approaches ten steps towards you. The rest He makes the devotee do with His help. That is His grace, His mercy.

* * *

178. That Ahimsâ (Non-injury) is the supremest virtue is no doubt true. But merely professing it by word of mouth is worse than useless; merely refraining from killing animals, as for example, not taking fish or meat, is not Ahimsâ. True non-injury can only be practised when God is seen in all beings, that is, when the Self is realised. The very nature of living necessarily involves at every moment, whether knowingly or unknowingly, destruction of or injury to the lives of countless beings, visible and invisible. The Yogis practise austerities by living upon milk, because it is a purely Sâttvic food. But to obtain that milk the calf which has its birthright to the whole of its mother's milk, has to be deprived of a part of its natural food. Is this not an act of injury or cruelty? But the more one can live without consciously injuring or harming others, so much the better. However, by

the habitual practice of real non-injury, one develops love for all beings, the little ego or selfishness disappears, and no distinction is felt between friend and foe. Consequently the heart is purified, and in the pure heart, God is fully reflected.

* * *

179. Sri Ramakrishna has said, "You should meditate in a corner, or in the forest, or in the mind." That helps the mind to be easily concentrated. "In a corner" means in a private, secluded spot. Spiritual practices should be done in privacy. For if they are done publicly, or with the knowledge of many people, various hindrances and obstructions arise. One's inmost feelings, or modes of spiritual practice, should be kept hidden; gushing outward expression destroys them almost before they can take root. The more you keep within yourself your spiritual sentiments and devotion, the more they grow and increase in intensity. For this reason the Sâttvic Sâdhaka practises Japa and meditation alone in darkness, or at the dead of night, or in bed inside the mosquito-net, so that

nobody may come to know of it.

*   *   *

180. "In the forest" means in a solitary
spot far away from the noise of men and
cities, as for example, in the Himalayas,
or on the banks of holy rivers like the
Gangâ, or in a pure and healthy atmosphere amidst the beauties of nature. Yogis
choose spots such as these, as favourable to spiritual practices, where there
is not the least occasion for temptations like "woman and gold". But if one
continues to think of worldly matters, even
after retiring into the forest, then it no
longer remains a forest; it is as good as
taking the world along with you. But if
the mind can be stilled and made one-
pointed, nothing external can disturb its
balance. Then this market-place of the
world becomes a forest to the Yogis, just
as he feels the stillness of the forest even
in the midst of the uproar of the market-
place.

*   *   *

181. Meditation "in the mind" is the
essential thing. Wherever you may meditate, install the chosen Ideal in the inmost

recesses of your heart, and restraining the senses, apply all your strength to concentrating the entire mind or the ego-consciousness on it. Uninterrupted practice of this kind unfolds tremendous Soul-power within, by which the true nature of God can be realised. The more the mind is scattered in different directions, the more it loses its potential power and becomes weak and impotent, so that no great work can be achieved by it.

* * *

182. Meditate in darkness with closed eyes. Keep the windows open, so that the room may not be stuffy. Keep your clothing loose. The Master instructed some Sannyâsin disciples of his to meditate sitting naked, in order to develop the feeling of a child and a sense of freedom from bondage.

* * *

183. At the time of meditation one can conceive of the heart as the place of the chosen Ideal, in any of the various ways as one pleases, for example, as the *seat* of the heart, the *lotus* of the heart, the *cave* of the heart, the *temple* of the heart, the *sky*

or *ether* of the heart, or *vacuity* of the
heart, the *casket* or *sheath* of the heart,
the *centre* of the heart, the *abode* of the
heart, the *cottage* of the heart, the *arbour*
of the heart, the *throne* of the heart—
indeed in as many forms as the poetic
imagination of the aspirant may conceive.
Heart means one's inmost core of consciousness where, in ordinary parlance, the
lover's intense feeling of sweetness longs
to hold the beloved in passionate embrace.
One who cannot meditate keeping the
chosen Ideal within the heart can, in the
preliminary stage, meditate with a picture
or image form in front of himself; but
that is external.

*   *   *

184. The most favourable times for
meditation are: (1) the junction of the
day and night, that is to say, just at dawn
and at dusk; (2) at the "moment of
Brahman" as it is called, namely, the latter
part of the night, an hour before sunrise;
(3) at the dead of night. During these
hours Nature is still, peaceful and solemn.
And during these hours the Sushumnâ
nerve which is inside the spinal column

generally becomes active, and as a consequence the breathing is done through both
the nostrils. At other times, one or other
of the two nerves, Idâ and Pingalâ, which
run on the two sides of the Sushumnâ,
is active, and breathing is done either
through the right or the left nostril. This
makes the mind unsteady. Many Yogis,
for this reason, watch when the Sushumnâ
becomes active, and as soon as they find
this out they sit for meditation, throwing
aside all work.

*   *   *

185. There are times when the aspirant
feels that the mind is dull and monotonous,
and no feeling or idea animates it; there
is no inclination to do Japa or meditation;
or the mind drives headlong towards lower
thoughts and tendencies, and it does not
seem possible to halt it by any amount of
effort. If it continues like this, then the
only remedy is holy company. By coming
in contact with holy persons, by their sight
and touch, and by personal service to them,
their spirit and divine mood are transmitted
to the heart of the devotee, bringing spiritual urge and inspiration, the dross of

the mind is washed away, and one goes forward with new enthusiasm. If there be no opportunity for holy company, recourse should be had to the study of the sacred scriptures, discussion of good topics, and prayer to God with a yearning heart. A firm resolve should also be made to repeat His name or the Mantra, whether one likes it or not, and to exercise one's will-power. It will then be found that the devil has taken to his heels, and the murky night of Tamas has melted away.

* * *

186. Keep the mind always engaged in some work or other; never allow it to remain idle; for no sooner do you leave it unemployed, than it will at once make mischief and pester you. Whenever you find the mind unduly restless or overcome with evil thoughts, or discover that you are unable to resist some temptation, or to put down mental excitement in spite of struggle, then leave the place and get away from that adverse atmosphere which may ultimately degrade you. Even if you go out and walk briskly three or four miles in the open air of the country-side, the

downward tendency will be checked at
least for the time being. There are only
two ways of saving oneself from temptation—either fight or flight. But, alas! there
is no way to flee and remain away from
the mind; either it must be brought under
control, or one must get up and down at
its bidding.

*　　　*　　　*

187. As friction brings out the fire which
is in wood, churning, the butter which is
in milk, grinding, the oil which is in
sesame, digging, the water that is under-
ground—even so, the Supreme Self which
lies hidden in the cave of the heart manifests Itself in Its true nature to the Jiva as
his essence, by austerities and concentration
of the mind performed with whole-souled
devotion.

*　　　*　　　*

188. In the first stage of spiritual practice, meditation and Japa should be increas-
ed slowly and gradually. If you devote,
say, half an hour or three quarters of an
hour today, do one hour after a few days
or weeks; next, go on steadily increasing it to one-and-a-half, two, and so on

by slow degrees according to ability. If, due to an excess of eagerness or feverish excitement of mind to gain quick result, you suddenly proceed by sheer force and strain yourself to do more than you are physically and mentally capable of, you have to suffer afterwards the dire consequences of your rashness. The reaction is so terrific that it is extremely difficult to bear it. As a consequence, nervous debility or exhaustion sets in so severely that even the capacity and the will to practise Japa and meditation disappear and the head or the brain feels empty, as it were, and does not respond. Then it requires much time and care and entails much hardship to recover the former state. The brain might even become deranged. It is not possible to reach the roof at one bound; that would mean falling down and breaking one's limbs. To climb to the roof, one has to go up the stairs step by step.

*   *   *

189. Those who practise intense Japa and meditation, or Yoga, develop a new Sâttvic body and a finer nervous system and subtle nerve centres which are capable

of bearing the force of profound supersensuous ideas and emotions.

*　　　*　　　*

190. To reecive full provisions or take a full meal from a Satra or feeding-house for mendicants, is forbidden to Sannyâsins. Householders who amass wealth, generally by trade, donate big sums of money to these Satras at the time of Shrâddha-ceremonies, with a view to the well-being of their ancestors in after-life, or for the purpose of remission of their own sins, or to accumulate Punya, or religious merit, or with the desire of gaining various worldly objects. Hence the food of the Satras is spiritually polluted, and this makes the mind impure and degrades it. Mâdhukari-Bhikshâ, that is, begging morsels of cooked food from a number of dwelling-houses, as a bee collects honey from different flowers, is the best for Sannyâsins; the food obtained by such begging is pure.

*　　　*　　　*

191. Unless Sannyâsins go on doing spiritual exercises properly, they have no right to accept gifts from householders. That would be practising deception upon

the householders, and this would detract
the Sannyâsins from their life of holy
vows. Householders serve Sannyâsins with
the view that they may spend all their time
upon spiritual practices without having to
worry about food, clothing and other bare
necessaries of life. By reason of this meritorious action they naturally come to have
a share of a portion of the fruits of the
spiritual practices and merits of the Sannyâsins. For this reason Sannyâsins should
earn sufficient merit to leave enough for
themselves, even after deduction of the
portion due to their donors and benefac-
tors. Otherwise, if they become bankrupt,
they themselves will morally and spiritually
suffer great loss. There is no end to the
misery of those who are bankrupt, here
and hereafter. They are chronically in
want. That is why Sannyasins with the
spirit of true renunciation, as well as ortho-
dox and pious Brâhmins, never accept gifts,
just as Sri Ramakrishna's father never
accepted them. Apart from that, the acceptance of gifts entails a sense of obligation and
so curtails one's freedom.

*   *   *

192. A person becomes a Brahmachâri
or a Sannyâsin for the sole purpose of
realising God in this very life after aban-
doning his duty to and responsibility for
parents and family. This makes them a
sharer of a part of the merits of his spiritual practices. So it is said, "Hallowed is
the ancestry and blessed is the mother" of
a man of true renunciation. That itself
repays the son's debt to the parents. But
if a Sannyâsin, who has caused his parents
to shed tears by leaving them, falls from
the ideal and spends his days idly or in
vain activities and evil ways, then all his
meritorious acts are washed away by their
tears. The only atonement for such a fall
is to go back to the life of the householder
and to fulfil the duties of that life.

*　　*　　*

193. Only the realisation of God makes
one's fund of spirituality inexhaustible, like
the pot of milk of the child Gopal. The
milk neither empties itself nor diminishes
in the pot, however much one may pour it
out. You know the story, don't you? A
poor Brahmin widow's little son, Gopal,
had to go to a village school alone every

12

day through a forest. This used to make him very nervous. When he told this to his mother, she said: "Why, my child, why should you be afraid? Your Madhusudan Dâdâ (elder brother, Krishna) lives in the forest. He will come as soon as you call him." The boy, simple as he was, readily believed this and whenever he was afraid he would cry out, "Where are you, Madhusudan Dâdâ?" Immediately a little boy of charming appearance used to come out of the forest saying, "Here I am, my brother. What is there to be afraid of?" and he would accompany Gopal through the forest, talking and playing with him. Some days passed in this way and the boy was very happy. Now the time came for the Shrâddha ceremony for the welfare of the departed mother of the school teacher, and the students were told to bring various things as presents to him for the occasion. So all the students who had the means took various kinds of presents in generous quantities to their school teacher. But Gopal's mother had nothing to send. Madhusudan dâdâ, noticing that Gopal

was going to the school that day with a
doleful countenance, asked him the reason,
and consoling him gave him a small pot of
milk saying, "Take this to the teacher".
No sooner did Gopal give that to the
teacher than he flew into a rage and scold-
ed the boy severely for his trifle. But
all were struck with wonder to find that
as soon as the pot was emptied, it became
full again. Then, the teacher, hearing
everything from Gopal, went with him
into the forest and asked him to call his
Madhusudan Dâdâ so that he could see
him. As soon as Gopal called, a voice from
heaven was heard. "You see Me because of
your simple faith, but your teacher is not
qualified to see Me, because his mind is not
yet pure."

*　　*　　*

194. He alone who calls on God from
the heart with simple faith, and wants
nothing else besides Him, will find Him.
And finding Him, there remains nothing
else for him to want or to get. He who
calls on God for gaining happiness here
and hereafter, or who begs for worldly

things from Him, may get them if He so wills, but he does not find God Himself.

*   *   *

195. The reason of Brahmachârins and Sannyâsins falling from their Ideal is "Woman and Gold". Such is the amazing delusion caused by lust and wealth that it brings the downfall of even great Yogis and Jnânis. As a sapling is hedged round for its protection, so the scriptures contain many rigorous rules for guarding Sannyâsins and Brahmachârins. Tulsidas has said, "Where there is lust, there is no Rama". Kabir has said that the Yogi who has sexual intercourse with women is a cheat and a hypocrite. Sri Ramakrishna used to forbid his young disciples to associate with women—even with women devotees. He used to say, "Do not associate with a woman devotee, even if she sheds a flood of tears at the name of the Lord. *Her* mind may be pure, but impure thoughts may arise in *your* mind." It was actually found that some of those promising young boys who later in life failed to observe the Master's counsel slipped and

fell, even after they had attained high
spiritual states.

* * *

196. The Holy Mother's observations on
this subject are still more stern and startling.
She told an initiated young widow disciple
of hers, "My child, never trust the opposite sex. What to speak of others, do not
even put your trust in your father or
brother, nor even in God Himself if He
comes before you assuming the form of a
man!" The idea is that, so long as there
is the feeling of self-identification with the
body, there is also lust, and consequently
the danger of falling. So long as the mind
is immature, or unripe, there is always the
chance of its being carried away by temptation. One should therefore keep oneself
away from it by utmost endeavour; otherwise danger is inevitable.

* * *

197. For the aspirant there is no other
enemy so terrible and so difficult to conquer as lust. There is no escape from its
clutches without ceaseless struggle till
death. It is like the saying of Râvana's:
"What an enemy is this Rama! He dies

not even after being killed again and
again!" Our Puranas contain so many
stories about great Yogis and Rishis who,
after practising severe austerities for hundreds of years, · slipped from Brahmacharya, having succumbed to the infatuation of women. So the scriptures enjoin
that Sannyâsins and Brahmachârins should
not be on intimate terms with women;
they should not even look at their faces,
or talk in an unrestrained way or joke with
them in secret. They are directed not
even to look at the pictures of women; for
these may excite evil impulses in an immature mind and create bad tendencies
which act in a subtle way. Stringent rules
such as these are, however, not meant for
the average person, but only for Sannyâsins and Brahmachârins who, having renounced everything, seek to realise God
in this very life by the practice of Yoga and
severe austerities. They belong to a different category.

*   *   *

198. For this reason, a religious aspirant
should shun like poison free and promis-
cuous mixing with the opposite sex. All

religious organisations and institutions, ancient or modern, where this rule has been violated, suffered pollution and degradation. Instances of this are found in the Buddhist, Tântric and Vaishnava sects in India, and in the Roman Catholic Orders of the West in the Middle Ages. When a nunnery for Bhikshunis (nuns) was founded in Buddha's time, he remarked: "The seed of the destruction of Buddhism has now been planted!" The great teacher of Divine Love, Sri Chaitanya, despite his limitless mercy, abandoned his beloved monastic disciple, the younger Haridas, for the simple reason that he had accepted alms from the hands of one of his Master's most eminent lady devotees. What a severe lesson for the instruction of humanity!

* * *

199. The only way to drive away lust from the mind is, for men to look upon all women as their mothers, and for women to look upon all men as their children. Unless this mental attitude is cultivated, there is every chance of a fall. And unless lust is controlled and strict Brahmacharya

is observed, the mind never becomes quiet, perfect meditation and one-pointedness are not attained, and Râgânugâ Bhakti, or Supreme Love for God, as distinguished from formal devotion, is not acquired.

*   *   *

200. The unripe mind is a great deceiver. It is very difficult to understand when and how, in an unguarded moment, it may unconsciously lead the aspirant astray and bind him in the meshes of Mâyâ. The nature of the unripe mind is to seek the pleasures of the body and the senses; to be infatuated by the Mâyâ or attachment to wife, children and family, thinking them to be its own; and to regard wealth, progeny, fame, position and power as the only desirable objects of life. It does not come to its senses even after repeatedly suffering pain in the search for pleasure and receiving blows at every step. The man with an unripe mind, even after seeing every day that people are dying on all sides, does not realise that he himself will also have to depart at any moment, leaving everything behind. He wants to secure his own ends ingeniously, indeed, by

any means whatsoever; it does not matter in the least to him whether his actions cause loss or suffering to others. His own happiness is all that he cares for. His whole interest is centred in this world.

* * *

201. The unripe mind is like unsmelted ore from a mine, full of dross and impurities of all kinds. If the original rough material is washed and smelted according to chemical processes, it can be converted into pure gold or into other things far more valuable even than gold, and these serve and help man in many ways. Similarly, the unripe mind can be made pure, if it is washed with the water of Viveka, that is, discrimination between the Real and the unreal; if its desire for worldly objects is burnt away by the fires of renunciation and love of God; and if it is purified by the practices of spiritual discipline as taught by the Guru for the attainment of the Highest Truth. Then the unripe mind becomes ripe. The Ever-pure Supreme Lord, Who is of the nature of Existence, Consciousness and Bliss, manifests Himself in that pure, ripe mind.

202. The mind is like a fruit. An un-ripe fruit tastes sour, astringent or insipid, and causes all sorts of illness if eaten; but when it is ripe, how sweet and beneficial it is! Then it can even be offered to God in worship. So, also, is it with the mind.

*   *   *

203. The unripe mind may be Sattvic, Rajasic or Tamasic. Those who have the Sattvic mind are religious by nature. They have a keen desire to realise God, to walk along the path of righteousness and to do good to others. They strive also to acquire these qualities, but due to various reasons, such as misfortune, physical unfitness, or their thinking themselves weak and in-competent, they do not advance far and easily lose heart. Those who have the Rajasic mind are so much engrossed with the world and worldly pursuits that they do not bother themselves much about reli-gion; or they pretend to be religious or, at the utmost, try to make the best of both worlds. Those who have Tamas are mostly the evil-doers. Their only thought and endeavour is how to injure and ruin others.

They are lustful, greedy—sinners.

* * *

204. Persons of an unripe mind who devote themselves to doing good to their country or to the world, or who build up institutions for allied purposes, do more harm than good to the world in the long run despite their lofty aims. They cannot long remain faithful to their higher ideals amidst the various blows and counter-blows of the world; they succumb to temptations in spite of hard struggles. The desire for name, fame, position and power grows strong in them; while jealousy, hatred, narrowness and selfishness get such a hold over them that all their work ends in smoke. Not only that, but by infecting society with the poison which is within them, they even corrupt many well-meaning persons, and arouse suspicion and mistrust in the public mind towards all philanthropic works and religious bodies and institutions, and even against religion itself.

* * *

205. In the beginning there was Brahman without a second, the Pure Exist-

ence immersed in Its own glory. He was alone, nothing else existed. All was well. Then, in an unguarded moment, He desired, "I shall be many", and there came into being the whole creation with its myriads of worlds! And even He had to perform austerities and meditation to accomplish this. Having created the universe, comprising all the movable and immovable objects—all the animate and inanimate objects—He Himself entered into them, and endowed man alone with reasoning faculties. His consequent plight, as the saying goes, was, "Brahman weeps, caught in the meshes of the five elements". Now, these so-called wise 'many" consider themselves free of all personal responsibilities, having shifted all their faults and errors, follies and foibles, incapacities and evil habits, and so forth, on to His shoulders! If they are unsuccessful in any work due to their own mistakes or lack of effort, they say, "It was not His will!" And if they fail to do something upon which they were very much bent, they merely say: "It happened so according to His will!" As if they have come to know everything, what the Lord wills and what He does not! If that be so, they must be no ordinary persons; they even know the mind of the Omniscient One! They also declare with a show of authority, "It is the will of God that everyone should marry and live a worldly life. For, if all should take to holy orders, how would creation be sustained?" As if they are passing sleepless nights dreading this dire catastrophe— the dissolution of the world! As if all the people the world over were dying to become monks!

*   *   *

206. In common parlance we often use expressions like "It is God's will", or we call upon God to help, or to bear witness, or we swear in the name of God or Dharma. These are merely hollow words— empty sound and fury, signifying nothing. It is just like little children saying, "Upon my honour!" or like the English expressions: "By Jove!", "Thank God!", "My God!", "God alone knows!". He alone truly feels the Divine will and is entitled to say so, who has resigned himself completely to God, who has realised the

Truth: "I am the machine, He is the Mechanic"; who makes no distinction between good or bad, who has neither desire nor aversion for anything; and who remains the same in praise or blame, in gain or loss, in pleasure or pain.

* * *

207. According to the Vedas, that Brahman which is the Whole, is whole for all time; It neither increases nor decreases, neither waxes nor wanes. If the Whole be subtracted from the Whole, there still remains the Whole Itself; and even if the Whole be added to the Whole, the sum is that same Whole! And that is predicable only of Brahman which is the Whole—the Infinite Supreme Self. Wholeness is gained only in exchange for the Whole Itself. To realise the Supreme Lord who is the Whole by nature, the Absolute, one must devote to the task the fullest capacity of body, mind, heart and soul, and strive to lose himself in Him. Then only the desired end is attained.

* * *

208. But all do not have the same

strength and ability. To a hardy, sturdy
and talented youth who has sundered all
his ties with the world and who practises
Yogic exercises day and night, in solitude,
for controlling the mind and stopping all
mental modifications, who lives upon one
meal a day by begging, or upon chance
roots and fruits, attainment of God or
Samadhi may be easy. But there are others
who in spite of their intense longing for
Realisation, find themselves always in extremely unfavourable situations. They are
occupied in the world in serving helpless
and aged parents, or are engaged in bone-
breaking toil to maintain wife and children.
And there may also be devotees confined
to bed with some incurable illness, their
body and mind too exhausted to perform
spiritual exercises properly. Is there no
hope of salvation for such? Will they
continue to be rocked and knocked about
for all eternity upon the tumultuous sea of
cause and effect, like a small boat caught
in a storm? Have they no hope of deliverance? Will they be mercilessly crushed
by the results of their past Karma, like
worms and insects, under the inexorable

wheel of cause and effect? No, this can
never happen in the domain of a merciful
God. Their heart-rending cries are sure to
reach His ears, and they will assuredly hear
within their hearts the still, small voice of
hope and consolation. If their desire for
Mukti is deep and strong, and they take
refuge in God with a yearning heart,
knowing full well their own incapacity; if
they lead a domestic life performing all
work without attachment and from a sense
of duty, and regarding their family and
kinsfolk and everything as belonging to
God; and if they are not bound to any
work, or by any attachment or infatuation
for any persons, and do not love anybody
from the heart except God—then, however
adverse the circumstances and environment
may be, they too will become heirs to peace
in this life and gain the Supreme State
hereafter, out of the boundless grace and
mercy of the Lord Who is Love personified, Who frees His devotees from the fetters of fate.

*   *   *

209. Everything is the working of the
mind, everything depends upon the mind

alone. Freedom is in the mind alone,
bondage is in the mind alone. As is the
tendency of the mind, so is its movement
towards action. If the above-mentioned
Yogi should in course of time be attracted
by worldly pleasures or by name and fame,
under the influence of desires stowed away
in his subconscious self, then, despite his
practice of severe austerities, and circumstances favourable in every way for it, all
his spiritual disciplines and hardships would
be no more than fruitless toil, like pouring
melted butter on ashes. But if an individual
afflicted by the threefold misery (material,
mental and providential) realises in the
core of his being the unreality of the
world, and consequently being averse to
all passions and attachments, resigns himself to God with all his heart and soul,
then in that case, He delivers him from
the cycle of birth and death—the root of
all misery.

*   *   *

210. Whether you be a Sannyasin or a
householder, you have to strive your utmost
along your own line, you have to build up

your entire life in harmony with your spiritual path. Realisation cannot be had by trickery; one deceives only oneself by practising deception. Taking all in all, it seems as if God shows somewhat more favour to householder devotees than to Sannyasins. The latter have renounced everything for the sole purpose of calling on God alone. It is certainly a great sin if they ever fail to do so. But pious and unflinching householder devotees remember and think of Him and pray for His grace even while carrying their heavy burdens along the rugged road of the world. Moreover, they respect, honour and serve Sannyasins and devotees of God and perform meritorious acts like giving alms and founding charitable institutions for helping the poor and the distressed and rest-houses for pilgrims, and so on.

*   *

211. Realisation of God in this very life does not fall to the lot of everybody. Those who have been practising severe austerities and spiritual disciplines life after life for realising Him, and who have

only a little Karma left to work out, are born endowed with good tendencies and urges, by reason of the merit acquired in their previous lives. Thus, when they get favourable circumstances for spiritual effort in the present birth, they finish the rest easily and are merged in the Supreme State which is beyond birth and death.

* * *

212. There is no kind of work that does not produce results, or that is wasted or lost. Work will inevitably bear its fruit, good or bad, some time or other. For this reason what is good should by all means be done. Such action becomes itself converted into capital, out of which the debt of evil deeds and the accumulated mass of sin are paid off.

* * *

213. The fruit of good deeds is inexhaustible. The more it can be accumulated, the more it stands one in good stead in this life and in the next—in dangers, pain or bereavement, in struggles and temptations, in darkness, fear and despair. Other possessions are temporary; their acquisition

and preservation involve pain, their decay or loss causes pain; nor can a person take them along with him after death. Not only that, but the unsatisfied and suppressed desires for those things of attachment follow him in the next life in the shape of Samskaras, and cause unending miseries by forcibly entangling him into new work and to the fruits thereof, thus adding further and further bondages.

* * *

214. The individual soul imprisoned in the world is, Sri Ramakrishna used to say, like the green betel-nut or green cocoanut —its kernel sticks so fast within the hard shell that it seems to be one with it and cannot be separated. But when it ripens and is dried up, it separates easily. Similarly, as long as there is self-identification with the body, as long as a person feels himself happy or miserable due to the happiness or pain of the body, so long does he remain bound by Maya and suffer ceaselessly from the threefold misery. The Jiva becomes free only when, by God's grace, the realisation comes that the Self is separate from the body and the senses

and other internal organs. It is by the practice of the Yoga, of Knowledge, of Devotion, or of Work, that the Self is realised as Ever-pure, Ever-enlightened and Ever-free by nature, being the Absolute Reality.

* * *

215. The mind can be purified and Self-knowledge attained by Karma Yoga. Work we all do, but we do not practise Karma Yoga. That is why we get bound by work and suffer misery. The Divine Lord Sri Krishna says in the Gita in regard to Karma Yoga, that you have the right only to work but not to the fruits thereof. Again He says, "Wretched are they who work for results"—meaning that those whose incentive to work is to gain certain personal ends are small-minded people belonging to an inferior class. Work, but whatever you do, do it selflessly, without attachment; do it for its own sake, without expectation for reward. In that case you will be liberated from all bondage, you will have performed all your duty and achieved the aim of life, by being blessed with the attainment of Supreme Bliss

which is beyond happiness and misery.

* * *

216. To many it is a puzzle how a person can possibly feel the urge or inclination to work if there is no desire for fruit. How can we be engrossed in work by devoting all our mind and energy to it, and why should we work at all, if it brings us no gain whatsoever? It is a great mistake to think so. Of course it is true, men work for happiness; but how much or what sort of "happiness" do we manage to get that way? Nine-tenths is misery and one-tenth or perhaps less is happiness; and even that little is fleeting and adulterated with misery. And moreover, in order to gain any selfish end, one usually has to deprive others of their due, and so causes them suffering, pain and injury even. On the other hand, all happiness that is permanent in this world is achieved only by selfless and non-attached workers, those who do not feel that they are the doers of the work. How many truly selfless and indefatigable workers like Sri Krishna, Buddha, Jesus Christ, Sri Chaitanya, and Sri Ramakrishna and Swami Vivekananda

in modern times, have there been in the whole of history? Very few, indeed! They alone are the ideal men who have, from time immemorial, enabled countless men and women to carry on their shoulders the unbearable burden of life, and who have instilled hope and peace into the hearts of myriads of souls sunk in the mire of sin, covered by the darkness of ignorance, and afflicted by the threefold misery. Inspired by their precepts and ideals, millions of persons have scorned life and gave it up for others without quailing—and, in return, have earned deathless life.

217. Dispassion, non-attachment to worldly objects and love for all beings are the very fundamentals, the root-principles, of every religion. He who has these virtues is not subject to the body and the senses, has no desire for name and fame or love of power, has no egoistic idea of "I and mine", and no feeling of distinction between his own relations and others. He looks upon all living beings—rich and poor, Brahmin and pariah, virtuous and vicious, enemy and friend, animals, birds and

insects—with an equal eye. He is unaffected—neither elated nor depressed—by
praise or blame, gain or loss, victory or
defeat, pain or pleasure. Even working,
he does not work, and even without working, he works. He is, verily, the ideal
Karma-Yogi.

* * *

218. The aim of Pranayama is to control
the Prana, or the vital force which functions in the body. That vital force manifests itself to us as breathing (inhaling
and exhaling). If it can be made to flow
rhythmically, the natural restlessness of the
mind subsides and it becomes tranquil.
As the mind is scattered over various
objects, its powers are frittered away. If
all these scattered forces can be concentrated on any single object, then the mind
acquires infinite power. According to the
scriptures on Yoga, there is nothing in the
universe which is beyond the power of such
a mind to attain. If in the spiritual realm,
that concentrated power is directed by
means of meditation to the true nature of
the Supreme Self, the Jiva is merged in
the Supreme Brahman through Nirvikalpa

Samadhi, the highest Superconscious state. And if the mind becomes wholly absorbed in the contemplation of God-with-form in the lotus of the heart, one is blessed with the direct vision of the Chosen Ideal, that is, realises God. Furthermore, if it be applied to natural or supernatural phenomena, various subtle and wonderful truths concerning these are discovered, and the eight Siddhis, or superhuman faculties or occult powers, are acquired.

* * *

219. The eight Siddhis are: (1) Animâ, the power of becoming as small as an atom; (2) Laghimâ, the power of assuming excessive lightness at will; (3) Vyâpti, the power of being all-pervading at will; (4) Prâkâmya, irresistible will; (5) Mahimâ, the power of increasing one's size at will; (6) Ishitva, sovereignty; (7) Vashitva, the power of subjugating others to one's will; and (8) Kâmâvasâyitâ, the power of being able to act, or to obtain desired objects, at will.

* * *

220. These occult powers, or the eight Siddhis, are terrible temptations and

tremendous obstacles in the way of achieving Nirvikalpa or Savikalpa Samadhi, the
highest states attainable by the practice
of Yoga. If the Sadhaka, or aspirant,
succumbs to the temptation of acquiring
these powers, he not only slips from the
path of Yoga, dragged down by desires,
but becomes depraved by their misuse and
indulges in carnal pleasures and, worst of
all, effects the ruination of many innocent
souls in order to gain his own selfish ends.
As a consequence he brings about his own
downfall and the powers themselves are
also lost to him.

*   *   *

221. The exclusive practice of Yoga is
extremely difficult and is not meant for the
average person. Especially, under modern
conditions, it is well-nigh impracticable
to observe strictly the necessary rules, e.g.
Sattvic and light food (such as fruits,
roots and milk), moderate exercise and
sleep, a lonely spot with pure air to live in,
a life without worry, regularity in everything—above all, the strictest continence
and restraint of the senses, and living near
or with one's Guru who must be an adept

in Yoga. It is extremely difficult to succeed if any one of these injunctions is violated. Also, if there is some error or flaw in the observance of the process prescribed by the Guru, or if one practises Yoga according to one's own idea by reading books, there is the chance of contracting some incurable nervous disease or heart trouble, and it may even lead to insanity or derangement of the brain.

* * *

222. Why and when does breathing (inhaling and exhaling) become uneven, that is to say, very rapid or very slow? Whenever we are overcome by passions like lust, anger, etc.; when we become bewildered by running after objects of enjoyment in the hope of pleasure; when we lose self-control in anger if someone puts an obstacle in our path of gaining our desired objects, or sink in despair if we fail; when we are inflated with pride at success, lose all sense of propriety due to infatuation, or turn green with envy at the sight of the good of others; when the heart sinks in fear of impending dangers, or is smitten with anxiety at the thought of some

approaching calamity; when we get despondent from want, and feel worried for
the maintenance and safety of wife and
children, or become restless and tormented
by illness; when we see darkness everywhere due to grief caused by the loss of
our dear ones, or turn mad, as it were, at
the loss of wealth and property—then it is
that the mind is involuntarily thrown into
a state of terrific agitation, and simultaneously breathing either becomes quick, like
fast hammer blows, or so slow that it seems
as if it is going to stop. This terrific agitation of the mind also agitates the Prana,
or vital force, and disturbs the blood circula-
tion. Unless the root-cause of all these be
removed, that is, unless one develops non-
attachment or dispassion to worldly objects,
it is altogether impossible to commune with
the Self, or to practise Japa and meditation with one-pointedness of the mind,
however much one may pray to God or
practise Pranayama.

* * *

223. There are many who think: "I
have not much attachment for the body;
I do not have much passion for my wife,

or fondness for my children, nor much attraction for money; I am not bound to anything; I could easily shake it all off if I willed." But when they reel under blows and counterblows from within and without, or are tossed up and down faced with some horrible ordeal by a turn of fortune, then they are roused from their delusion and realise their hopeless plight of being bound hand and foot by the terrible fetters of Maya. Those who are endowed with good tendencies inherited from previous births find these fetters intolerable. They strive heart and soul to get free of them by any means whatever. These are the Mumukshus, that is, persons desirous of attaining Mukti, or freedom from birth and death.

* * *

224. There is another class of Jivas who lead a life of subjection like bondslaves, generation after generation. Their condition becomes so natural to them that they are afraid even to hear the name of freedom. They think: "We are all right as we are. If we have to enter upon the road to freedom which is unknown and uncertain,

renouncing all that we have, we would rather forgo freedom!" If the worm which lives in filth is placed on a heap of flowers, it dies panting for breath. These are the bound-Jivas. They remain eternally bound to the worldly life.

*   *   *

225. If the world were one of unbroken happiness, if there were no disease, bereavement, sorrow, want, dangers or calamities, fear or anxiety, who would have felt prompted to call on God? The Lord has given these for our instruction, for testing us, so that men may not remain forgetful of Him and may take refuge in Him realising their utter helplessness. So cling to Him by all means in all conditions, in happiness as well as in sorrow. Love Him with all your heart, and know Him to be your only goal, your sole support and resource, your all-in-all. You will then find that pain, sense of bereavement and evil will be unable to disturb the mind, and that the heart will remain filled with bliss.

*   *   *

226. Be a hungry beggar, hungry for the love of God. Weep yearningly for the

vision of His form of Love. Be mad for
Him as if life is unbearable without Him.
Who else is there who feels as He does the
distress of His devotee? Who else is one's
very own, as He is? Who else is after
one's heart—to whom one can lay bare
his whole heart and soul—as He? If one
repents, He pardons and takes one in His
lap in loving embrace, even after a hundred
transgressions. His love passeth all understanding, and is beyond all bounds. He is
the ocean of infinite happiness. He is the
ocean of the nectar of immortality. Jump
into that ocean and you will attain immortality, you will swim in bliss as *rasagollâ*
(a spongy sweet) floating in syrup. Is it for
nothing that the lover of God does not
want Mukti or Nirvana (Annihilation),
forgoing the enjoyment of bliss in the
worship of the Personal God?

*   *   *

227. The God-intoxicated, like drunkards, are of two classes: those who call
out "Mâ, Mâ", "Mother, Mother", singing
devotional songs of Shyâmâ, the dark-
coloured Divine Mother, with tears in their
eyes—and those others who drink so deep

that they become unconscious; they are not
satiated until they reach that condition.
The first named belong to the Bhakta class,
the second to the type of the Jnânin. Both
become wholly absorbed in spiritual moods
according to their respective attitudes. But
the devotee retains the attitude of "I am
His", and the Jnânin merges his ego in
Him in the thought of "I am He—I myself
am the unconditioned, infinite Existence,
Consciousness, Bliss, the Supreme Self, the
Brahman Absolute." Can you say whose
joy is greater? The final stages of Jnana
and Bhakti are one and the same; it is a
feeling of unity with the Self, where the
two intermingle, and the one cannot be
distinguished from the other.

* * *

228. The Formless Brahman is not like
the vastness of the Akâsha, elemental sky
or space. It is of the nature of Undivided
Consciousness. This Consciousness is all-
pervading—permeating everything through
and through. The existence of all objects
in the universe is due to Its Being, to Its
Existence therein; all knowledge of the
world comes from the light of Its Con-

sciousness, of Its Pure Intelligence; all happiness that is in creation flows from Its Bliss. The Brahman is *Virât*, immeasurably vast in this sense. The sky or the infinite space is merely a symbol for the convenience of meditation.

*　　　*　　　*

229. "The process for pouring oblations in the fire is Brahman, the clarified butter for oblations is Brahman, Brahman Itself offers oblations into the fire of Brahman. He who is absorbed in action, by seeing Brahman in it, attains Brahman Itself."— Gita, IV. 24. The import of this verse of the Gita is, that whatever is done should be done by looking upon everything as Brahman, that is to say, identifying oneself with Brahman or God. His whole life becomes an act of Yajna, or sacrificial worship, in which the process of oblation, the offering, the fire, the doer of the sacrifice, the work and the goal are all Brahman. Look upon all work as a Yajna, as His worship alone. While eating, think He Himself is the food, that the process of eating is also He, that He is also the instrument of eating, that is, the organs

14

with which we eat, and that, in fact, He
is the eater or the enjoyer of action. Eat
with the idea or feeling that you are
pouring the food as an oblation into the
gastric fire which is Brahman. Why only
to eating—you have to apply this idea of
Brahman or God to everything in the
world, to every act and to every thought.
Thus only the whole Karma of a person
engaged in work melts away, since his
Karma produces no other result than the
attainment of Brahman. That we may install
God in all our actions, in all our aims; that
we may feel His beneficent touch, His
benign will always and in everything; that
we may offer all the fruits of our actions,
good and bad, to Him, renouncing the
egoistic feeling of "I am the doer", is
what the Lord Sri Krishna teaches us in
this verse. It is recited in chorus before
meals at nearly all the branches of our
Belur Math (monastery).

*   *   *

230. There is a fine song of Ramprasad
embodying the same idea:

"O my Mind, I say unto you, worship
    Kâli by whatever rites it may

please you,

While repeating day and night the
divine Mantram of great power
given by the Guru.

When you lie down, think you are
making prostration to the Mother,

While you sleep, think you are meditating on Her.

While you go about the town, think
you are circumambulating the
Mother Shyâmâ.

Whatever enters your ears is verily
the Mantram (sacred name) of the
Mother.

Kâli is made up of all the fifty letters*
of the alphabet, every letter is a
name of Hers.

Partake of all kinds of dainty dishes
that are in the world—

Which are fit for chewing, sucking,
licking or drinking,

And think that you are offering oblation to Mother Shyâmâ."

*   *   *

---

* The vowels, consonants and compound letters of
the Sanskrit alphabet.

231. This body is transient, it will turn
into worms and ashes in the end after
death; its constituents are impure, loath-
some and filthy materials, such as, faeces,
urine, phlegm, blood, fat, marrow, flesh,
etc., and yet how foolishly the Jiva is
deluded by being imprisoned in such a
cage of bones and flesh! Being dreadfully
attached to this body and identifying himself with it, he suffers endless pain every
moment; but in spite of it he is not roused
to his senses. Such is the Maya of Maha-
maya, the Great Mother of Universal
Illusion! What a magic spell She has cast
over all! Those who aspire after Moksha,
or Liberation, should cut asunder this
utterly ruinous snare of delusion, knowing
the body and all the objects of the senses
to be unsubstantial and impermanent, and
strive to take refuge in the Eternal.

*　　　*　　　*

232. Sang a Bengali Sâdhaka-poet:
Such is the Maya of Mahamaya,
What a magic spell She has cast over
all!
Even the immortals, the Gods Brahmâ
and Vishnu,

Lie prostrate, unconscious, enthralled,
Unable to fathom Her!
What to speak of mortal man!
The cage-trap is set in a morass,
Or where the water flows out of a
tank,
The small fry enter it.
The passage of escape is always open,
But still they cannot get out.
The silkworm spins its cocoon,
It can escape out of it, if it will,
But being charmed by Mahamaya,
It dies in its own larva!
It perishes in the prison of its own
creation!

*   *   *

233. *Upâsanâ* means act of approaching
God, through worship, prayers and Service;
literally, to be seated in His proximity.
Vain thoughts and vain actions, far from
benefiting us, do us harm. Indulging in
them, we lose ourselves and they take us
away from God to a garbage pit, as it
were—indeed, nobody knows where. The
more we keep ourselves away from worthless thoughts and actions and from impermanent worldly objects, and devote our-

selves to the remembrance and contemplation of God, to meditation, worship and repetition of His holy name, and to activities like doing good to others and serving humanity, the closer we approach God, the more we are transfigured into His likeness, and the more are our hearts filled with bliss. There is no other way than this to conquer the world and to be saved from misery and mental disquietude.

*　　　*　　　*

234. At the Baranagore Math* I heard from the revered Swami Premananda two parables of Sri Ramakrishna, which I have not seen published anywhere. This is the first one: "Persons who belong to the class of Acharyas, or teachers, with special divine authority and mission are, 'ripe' or mature counters, as it were, in a game of drafts, whose moves for quickly reaching the goal are inevitable; but they purposely come down from the goal and play again. They know that with their master-strokes

---

* The first Monastery established in a rented house near the Cossipore garden-house after the passing away of Sri Ramakrishna there in 1886.

they can throw at will any number—two, four, six, eight, or ten. They pair with other 'green' or unreturned counters and take them to the goal also. Try to get paired. Nobody can destroy the pair in a play at dice. Likewise, there is no longer any fear if one gets a Guru like that."

* * *

235. The second parable runs as follows: "A hag had a pair of gold bracelets on her arms, which she had had made after denying herself much. But nobody came forward to speak in high terms of them. At last being disappointed, she set fire to her own hut, and having collected a crowd around her by yelling and sobbing with tears in her eyes, she began to lament pointing with her hands, 'Alas! Look you all, my hut has caught fire. Woe to me, all that I have is being burnt to ashes, only this pair of my bracelets is left.' In the same way, persons of mean nature become anxious to show off what little they may possess, or what little skill or power they may have acquired, even though they may thereby cause loss to themselves."

* * *

236. The whole life of a man is a mass of temptations. The six passions like lust, etc. are ever awake; they are ever on the look-out for anyone whom they can entrap and devour. One must, therefore, be always awake and alert, must always discriminate between right and wrong, and pray to God. If a thief finds light burning in a room and someone awake there, he does not break into the house, but goes away elsewhere. The moment you slacken, become careless or weak, your enemies also, finding an entrance, will grow violent and try to fell you with all sorts of crafty means; and even if they suffer defeat over and over again, they will never give in or fall back. But by no means lose heart. Even if you fall down again and again, you must get up every time with new vigour and fight with all your might and main. You will then find that even your defeat, if it be, is as good as victory. This will advance you a little further on your way every time. God Himself helps those who are sincerely eager to lead a higher life; He gives them strength and inspiration and makes the path smooth for them by

removing all sorts of obstructions, dangers and difficulties. And when, exhausted by ceaseless fighting with the passions, they take refuge in Him with a yearning heart, then He also takes them on His lap. For, His name is—"Compassionate towards the devotees".

* * *

237. Does the devotee serve God, or God the devotee? There comes a time when the devotee feels that what little service he can do to God is almost next to nothing, that it is God Himself who is really serving him. The worship of the devotee is like the worship of the Mother Gangâ with Gangâ water; that is, offering Him things which are His. The true Bhakta has no thought for himself; it is God who has to think about him. Whom do we call a Bhakta? It is he who has pure, desireless, unconditioned love for God, who is mad with love for God. God bears the burden of such a devotee, and provides for him whose whole heart and soul is ever fixed on Him. "To these I carry what they lack, and for them I preserve what they already have," says the *Gita*. Such devotees

are extremely rare. We read of them in
our Puranas and histories, e.g. Narada,
Prahlada, Shukadeva, Vidura, Sri Radha
and the Gopa-Gopis (Cowherds and Milkmaids) of Vrindaban, Uddhava, Mahavira
and others of the ancient epic age; and
Chaitanyadeva, Mirabai, Ramanuja, Tuka-
ram, Ramprasad of the historical period;
Ramakrishna, Vivekananda, Pavhari Baba,
Nag Mahasaya and others of the modern
times. Among these, Sri Radha, Sri Chaitanyadeva and Sri Ramakrishna are wor-
worshipped as Avataras or Incarnations of
God.

*   *   *

238. It is only because of his pure devotion and love that God submits Himself to
the devotee. He makes Himself over to the
devotee, indebted by the devotee's love and
acknowledges defeat on account of the
devotee's whole-souled love. God dwells
constantly in the heart of the devotee,
bound by the cord of love. Verily, there is
nothing that He cannot grant him.

*   *   *

239. As the devotee cannot live without
God, even so God Himself cannot live

without the devotee—like a young man and
a young woman in love. But the love
between a young man and his sweetheart
springs from lust and infatuation of each
other's beauty or accomplishments; it is
tainted with carnal desire. It reeks with
the "fishy" smell of personal happiness
and self-interest—it no longer endures if
there is any variation of these or incom-
patibility of temper, and it leaves a bitter
taste in the mouth. The love of God, on
the other hand, is desireless, supersensuous,
heavenly and everlasting. The more one
drinks that nectar of love, the more the
thirst for it grows; one never feels satiated.
Here Love, God of Love—the Beloved, and
the lover all become merged into one without distinction. Then what remains is—
Bliss Absolute.

*   *   *

240. Whatever be the manner of life or
situation in which the Mother may place
you, know that it is for your good—
whether you understand it or not. Happiness and pain are but the benign touch of
Her lotus hand. Who can comprehend
Her Lila (Sport)? Whether She keeps you

in happiness or misery, in weal or woe,
meekly accept everything as Her blessing.

"Even Mother's slaps and blows are
                                    sweet;
Let them fall on the back as much as
                            they may!
He who takes it in this sense,
Bravo! He is indeed a child of the
                                Mother.
The child does not die of Mother's
                                beating,
It does not fear Mother's frown.
It is content as Mother keeps it,
For, verily, it knows nothing besides
                            the Mother."

       *   *   *

241. What can you understand of God
by discussing scriptures, by logic-chopping,
by debating and reasoning with your two-
penny intellect? On the contrary, if you
try to comprehend Him by these means,
there is good chance of your getting con-
founded and coming to such a pass that
you may feel even doubtful about your
very existence. Since you have such a
rare thing as human life, will you spend
your days counting the leaves of the mango

tree and carrying on wonderful researches
about them, or will you satisfy yourself by
eating the mangoes? Let those who please
do such things; but Podo, my dear one,
you eat your fill of the mangoes.

*   *   *

242. To be sure, the pursuit of knowledge, analysis, reasoning and research and
the study of other sciences refine the intellect, bring to light many subtle principles
and lead to the discovery of many new
truths which do a lot of good to the world.
But this same knowledge and learning, in
the hands of selfish and materialistic people
or nations who think this world to be their
all in all, becomes the cause of endless
misery and destruction of human life, turns
men into savage beasts and the world into
a veritable hell.

*   *   *

243. Prayer is the act of making known
to the Lord or the Supreme Spirit—who,
residing in all beings, regulates their inner
feelings—the intense anguish or the want
or yearning of our heart, by means of profound thought or language, spoken or
unspoken, and the supplication for His

mercy to remove it. The prayer which is full of selfish desire says: "O Lord, I can no longer bear the torment, disease, bereavement, want and poverty of this life; do Thou make me happy, hale and hearty and take me beyond all want and worry." The desireless prayer is: "O Lord, put as much burden on my shoulders as Thou wishest, keep me in misery, throw me into danger, these do not matter in the least; but give me, O Lord, just this much strength and fortitude that I may not be perturbed by anything, that I may not forget Thee, that I may always have pure devotion to Thy lotus feet which dispel all fear."

* * *

244. The principal aim of human life is the realisation of God, or the attainment of Mukti. Man alone has the prerogative or the ability to attain this highest object of life—none else, not animals, not even Gods, or heavenly beings, can have it. It is denied to animals, because they are devoid of the faculty of discriminating between the Real and the unreal. Attainment of liberation is impossible for Gods, because they are too occupied with the continuous

enjoyment of the intense pleasure and splendours of heaven. What time is left for them for the practice of discrimination and renunciation? For this same reason, it is also difficult for those persons who own vast riches and much property to attain Mukti. Again, for those who are extremely poor and destitute and are ever tormented and perplexed, gnawed by hunger and driven by want, it is difficult to gain spirituality. Realisation of God is far easier for men of moderate means, because they stand between those two extremes. It is seen in the history of the world that nearly all the great personalities who have left an indelible impress on religion, society, polity and other fields of human activity or realms of thought, by the power of their genius, have been born of middle-class parents of moderate means—neither rich nor poor.

* * *

245. If today we fritter away our energies and quarrel among ourselves over what tomorrow may bring, we lose what might be gained both today as well as tomorrow.

* * *

246. Learning, intellect, knowledge of the scriptures, logic, argument, reflection, riches, charity, meritorious works, rituals and sacrifices, even Yoga and austerities— by none of these nor by all of these together can God be realised—not by any or all of these does He allow Himself to be captured, that is, apprehended. The only irresistible weapon for apprehending Him or holding Him captive is pure Love, whole-souled Devotion. "He is of the nature of ineffable Love." If you strike that chord, His nature will reveal itself, He cannot hide Himself any longer. It is like the milch-cow spouting milk in torrents, as it were, when the calf butts the udder with its head.

*   *   *

247. The Vedas have declared the Supreme God to be beyond all Gunas, or attributes; without the limitations of name and form, of time, space and causation; beyond the reach of language, mind and intellect; all-pervading, without beginning, without end, and inconceivable by nature. But the heart of the devotee never allows itself to be deterred by accepting all this— it cannot. The devotee says: "If God be

merely that alone, then what difference does it make whether He exists or not? Of what use is He to me if I cannot even see Him, if I cannot make Him my very own? Then, in vain are all spiritual practices and rites, I am in vain, and in vain also is this human life. What purpose is there in living? By all means, I must realise Him in this very life." The bitter weeping and wailing of the devotee's heart sways the throne of God; He cannot then remain unmoved any longer and dwell in His own majesty. He is, in truth, All-knowing, the Self of all beings, the Inner Guide of all, the ocean of unconditioned and spontaneous mercy, and above all, He is affectionate and loving to the devotee. So hiding His own real essence in order to satisfy the desire of the devotee's heart, He shows Himself in the form worshipped by him in the temple of his heart and fulfils his cherished end and aim of life. Further-more, from time to time He descends to earth assuming the human body, so that man may comprehend His true nature easily. When the Lord lives among men as an Avatara, or Incarnation, even the sinner and the afflicted find deliverance, through His grace, without rigorous spiritual practices or austerities.

* * *

248. God assumes form out of compassion for the aspirant and to make his worship easy. It is not possible to conceive of Him in His inconceivable aspect, which is beyond all attributes or limiting adjuncts, or to comprehend Him as the totality of all the abstract Divine qualities. Starting to model an image of Shiva, we often end by moulding a monkey! As long as we are human beings, as long as we have the sense of body or the sense of duality, so long we do not have any other alternative but to think of God as an Ideal Person endowed with infinite Divine attributes.

* * *

249. If we try to imagine God as without form, we can at best think of the vast sky or the limitless ocean. If we try to meditate on God in His Formless aspect in the initial stage, we can do no more than meditate on emptiness or void alone. Nothing can be superimposed on that—it is

like throwing stones in the dark. Meditation on the Formless Divine Father, or Formless Divine Mother is a laboured process of the barren imagination—a mere empty and meaningless phrase. We cannot proceed very far along the path of spiritual progress through formless meditation, because it is dry as dust and without any support to hold on to. The liberated Paramahamsa, who is devoid of the feeling of identification with the body, and who sees God in all beings, is alone qualified to meditate on the Formless Brahman beyond all limitations.

*　　　　*　　　　*

250. The Lord Sri Krishna says in the Gita, "I incarnate Myself in human body in every age for the deliverance of the good, for the annihilation of the wicked and for the resuscitation of religion when it is on the decline." But, says the Bhakta, this is only external, superficial; we have to proceed further and deeper. This is not all, there must be more to it. God is, indeed, all-powerful. He could have accomplished all this by mere will, without suffering endless misery by being embodied as an Avatara.

This alone cannot, therefore, be regarded as
the superexcellent proof of the Incarna-
tionhood of God. Krishna cannot be said
to be an Avatara merely because He killed
the wicked tyrants Kamsa and Shishupala,
who were revilers of religion. The history
of the world abounds with many such
incidents in which such tyrants have been
assassinated and their subjects freed from
oppression. Many miraculous events too
are seen in the lives of many Mahapurushas,
or great souls, who were pastmasters in
Yoga. They can work wonders; nothing
is impossible for them. The Incarnation-
hood of Sri Krishna is not proved even by
His actions as the King of Mathura or
Dwaraka, or even as the guide and helper
of the Pandavas in the battlefield of
Kurukshetra. He often had to resort to
questionable strategy in order to help them
achieve their object. Those wonderful
actions of his do, of course, arouse profound respect and amazement, and furnish
evidence of His marvellous versatile genius.
But they are nevertheless mere matters of
temporary or timely significance. They do
not exert any far-reaching, abiding influence

on the life of humanity.

*   *   *

251. The best proof of the Incarnation-hood of Sri Krishna is, verily, manifested by His Lila, or playful Sport, at Vrindaban, because therein alone He has revealed the real essence of His indescribable Love. How far pure devotion and love can submit God to the devotee, and how much He can make the devotee His own, are best understood from His Lila at Vrindaban. In that Lila of His, He has revealed to the world the peak of Love which is beyond the reach of our knowledge and intelligence. Attracted by that sublime Love, the young Gopis, or milkmaids, of Vraja (Vrindaban) used to run like mad to the banks of the Yamuna, hearing the call of His flute, in the hope of seeing Him and being near Him. Casting aside all sense of shame, fear, family reputation and social position, they used to lose in His company the sense of the body and their individuality and become merged in Him! Such a selfless love could never be evoked by any man but by God and God alone. The sweet, spiritual influence of that wonderful, Eternal and

ever-felt Divine Sport has been drawing the hearts of countless men and women for ages to their Beloved, aye, has been shedding peace and bliss on their lives, and qualifying them for Liberation, through worship of Him as their Chosen Ideal. Centuries after, the Great Master, Sri Chaitanya Deva, came down as an Incarnation to revive the idea of that very Love; and losing himself in *Mahabhava*, the highest blissful state of Samadhi, through contemplation of that sweet Sport of Sri Krishna with Radha, the chief of the Gopis, unstained by even the slightest taint of lust, he disseminated that divine love and pure devotion freely to one and all in the world. And in our own day, Sri Ramakrishna in singing or speaking of the same Lila of Radha-Krishna used to be so overwhelmed that he too lost himself in *Mahabhava*, expressing in his person all the outward eightfold signs of those rarest divine feelings which were manifested in the lives only of Sri Radha and Sri Chaitanya Deva.

*　　*　　*

252. One can renounce only what one

possesses; how can one renounce that which one does not have? If a thing is to be relinquished, it has first to be acquired. It will not do to shirk the trouble or the responsibility this entails. It will not do "to offer to Govinda the puffed paddy which has been blown away by the wind."*

The Shastras, or Hindu scriptures, do not forbid enjoyment; they say: "Enjoy the world through renunciation; that is to say, enjoy the world, giving up the feeling of 'mine' and attachment thereto. Everything in the universe is pervaded by God. He permeates every object, everything is His. Therefore, holding firm to this knowledge, do all work, enjoy everything, renouncing the idea of 'I and mine'; otherwise enjoyment will turn into suffering." If you enjoy the world with this idea, Yoga will come of itself; you will have practised it automatically, that is, without going through its prescribed processes.

*   *   *

* Govinda is a name of Sri Krishna. The allusion is to a shopkeeper who, seeing his popped paddy blown away by a gust of wind, and finding that it is all going to waste, offers it to Govinda with a

253. To think of and to remember the Ishta, or the Chosen Ideal means, establishing contact or union of the mind with Him. The deeper and the more uninterrupted the current of that thought flows to Him, the more the thoughts which scatter the mind-stuff* will quiet down, the more will the current be unbroken like the flow of oil poured into a vessel. Only then is it called Dhyana, or meditation. When that meditation deepens still further, the mind becomes one with the object of meditation; it becomes resolved into that form or substance. That state is called Samadhi, or the Superconscious state. Then only is the true nature of the Self fully experienced, the Chosen Ideal or God is realised. Only for that person who has realised Brahman, say the Upanishads, are the knots of the heart rent asunder, that is to say, all desires, etc. are destroyed, all doubts are

view to gain Punya, or religious merit in this or future life.

* Mind-stuff, *Antahkarana*. It is analysed by the Sankhya philosophy as *Manas*, mind or the receptive faculty, *Buddhi*, intellect or the determinative faculty, *Chitta*, or the cogitative faculty, and *Ahamkâra*, or the sense of ego.

for ever resolved, all the fruits of action are exhausted—verily, all misery ends. So it comes to this, that the first step for realising God is the constant thought and remembrance of Him; the calm, unruffled state of the mental modifications is the second step; Dhyana is the third step; Samadhi is the last step or rung of the ladder. It is not possible to reach a higher step by jumping over the previous ones. Thus the final stage of the constant thought and remembrance of God is the realisation of God.

*　　　*　　　*

254. Japa of the Mantra or of the holy name of God, meditation and worship have been prescribed in order that, by constant repetition and by the habit of continued practice, this thinking and remembrance of God may take firm root in the mind. For this reason alone it is necessary to repeat mentally the holy Mantra of the Chosen Ideal over and over again, daily, for a long time. The things with which we are continually occupied, or which we constantly reflect upon, leave their impression on the mind. Though they appear to

melt away from the mind, they remain there
in a subtle state, in the form of Samskaras,
or ingrained tendencies of the past; and as
soon as they find a favourable atmosphere
they prompt men unawares to thought or
action—in an evil way, if the bad tendencies
are strong, in a good way, if the tendencies
are good. It is therefore seen that evil-
doers gradually engage even more in evil
deeds, and those who are diligently struggling for spiritual progress advance rapidly in
that direction.

*   *   *

255. The sum-total of all the energy
that is in the universe remains always the
same; it neither waxes nor wanes, nor is
it annihilated. It has, however, modifications, or changes, and is transformed in
various ways—that is all. Nothing whatever of all that we do or think, good or bad,
is lost; it continues to be active in a subtle
manner, or is stored up and becomes active
as soon as the opportune moment arrives.
Thus, we ourselves have to reap the fruits,
good or bad, of our Karma, or work. Not
only that, this stored-up thought or action
of one also influences others and causes

them either suffering or hapiness.

* * *

256. Swami Vivekananda has said, that all the different kinds of forces of action and thought which we unconsciously broadcast in the world, continue to travel in wave-form through the space of the universe and act upon any person having the same vibrations, with whom they come in contact. They inspire him with the same idea, infuse strength into him, and they also themselves gather fresh impetus from him of like nature. Moreover, after completing the circle, that very force returns to its source of origin, with added strength. It is for this very reason, if we do somebody an injury, or inflict suffering on someone, we have to suffer similar conse-quences, some time or other, in this birth or in the next—this is the law of nature, none can escape it.

* * *

257. Because of our ignorance of this inexorable law of nature, and failing to find any direct or visible cause of our sufferings, we are unable to account for them with our ordinary intelligence, and

hence put all the blame on fate or some unseen Power, or on God and regard Him as cruel or partial. We are so enwrapped with delusion that we never for a moment reflect that we have to suffer the consequences of our own actions, perchance with compound interest! Therefore, reflecting upon these consequences, control all your acts and thoughts and guide them along the right path. Never be the cause of misery or injury to anybody for some temporary pleasure or gain. If you unswervingly follow the path of spirituality, you will inherit the *Daivi Sampads*,* or divine attributes spoken of in the Gita (XVI. 1-3). The mind will be purified, and you will perceive the action of Divine Force within your heart. You will then not be able to do wrong, even if you feel

---

* "Fearlessness, purity of heart, steadfastness in knowledge and Yoga, charity, control of the senses, Yajna, reading of the Scriptures, austerity, uprightness, non-injury, truth, absence of anger, renunciation, tranquillity, absence of calumny, compassion, uncovetousness, gentleness, modesty, absence of fickleness, boldness, forgiveness, fortitude, cleanliness, absence of hatred, absence of pride—these belong to one born for a divine state."

like doing it; as the Master Sri Ramakrishna used to say and literally verified in
his life, "You can never take a false step.
That alone is the sign of the supremely
spiritual person."

* * *

258. Many are under the impression that
Samadhi cannot be attained without the
practice of Yoga or treading the path of
Jnana or Knowledge. The Yoga philosophy of Patanjali speaks thus: "Union
with the Chosen Ideal is achieved, that is,
God is seen, by Mantra-japa or the repetition of the holy name." Just after this, it
is stated: "Samadhi is attained by self-
surrender to God"; also at another place,
it is said, "Or, by meditating on God."
That is to say, Samadhi can be had by
concentration of the mind on God or by
dedicating all actions and their fruits to
God. Moreover, the commentator, Vyasa-
deva, writes, in this context: "God being
pleased with the meditation of Him with
special love and devotion, shows favour to
the devotee by His mere wish. The Yogis
also attain Samadhi and its result very
quickly, merely by His wish," that is, un-

conditionally. So it comes to this, that the state of Samadhi can be reached even without practising the eightfold steps of Yoga. Attainment of absorption in God with form, and Samadhi in formless Brahman, are one and the same; only the attitude and the means vary; the realisation of the Reality and its effect are the same in both. In truth, that which is Brahman without attributes is Itself the Brahman with attributes; only, the worship of Brahman with attributes is easy for Jivas, or individuals, possessing as they do the sense of identification with the body.

*   *   *

259. Worship of God with a desire for some result is the worship of one's own self only, not of God. To call on God to be delivered from troubles and disease, misfortune and dangers, want, misery, fear, anxiety, bereavement and all such things, is for the sake of selfish gain or self-aggrandisement only, for the sake of one's own comfort and advantage. The aim of all codes and observances which are actuated by desire, like ritual bathing and

charity, external worship, religious ceremonies and festivals, vows and fasting. sacrificial and expiatory ceremonies, performance of rites to secure welfare and to avert possible evils, pilgrimages, service of holy people, recitation of the Chandi or Gita and so forth, is for getting rid of past sins and for accumulating religious merit. Getting rid of past sins means the desire to escape by some easy means from the torture of hell or the suffering of pain which is the inevitable evil consequence of sinful deeds committed previously—not the wish to exhaust the tendency to commit sin. The object of 'accumulating religious merit' is to live happily and in comfort in this life with relatives, children and family and to enjoy inexhaustible happiness in heaven hereafter! Both these desires are delusions of the mind—vain expectations. There is neither unmixed happiness in this world, nor eternal happiness in heaven. These are simply panegyrics or words of consolation or inducement recorded in the Scriptures, the Vedas, the Puranas, etc.— mere myths. These have been held forth to tempt those who are disinclined to the performance of religious duties and virtuous acts, by telling them: "Do this much only and you will have a millionfold result." It is just like a mother making the baby drink milk by diverting it with queer tales, or putting it to sleep by singing lullabies. The aim is good, no doubt, and the purpose is also served.

*　　*　　*

260. Should we then give up these forms of ritual worship and ceremonies because they are prompted by desire? Am I forbidding you to do them? Certainly not. Do them by all means, as long as your heart is so inclined. These observances broaden and cheer the mind, the Sattvic feeling or holy mood comes through good thoughts and the performance of good works, and they create faith in and attraction for higher religious duties and unselfish work. But at the same time remember that though they are, to be sure, Vedic injunctions, they belong to Karma Kanda, that section of the Vedas which relates to ceremonial acts and sacrificial rites—and they are not truly Bhakti, or devotion. In the love of God

there is no buying and selling, no shop-keeping or bargaining, no calculating of loss or profit, and no desire for fruits of action. Only there is the entire dedication of body, mind and soul, and everything else, to the God of the heart; there is the fullest satisfaction simply in loving Him— because when He is loved, no other object of desire is found to be worth seeking. It is love for Love's sake. The very nature of such a devotee is to love; his whole attitude is, "I cannot bear to live and breathe without loving Him." This is the final stage, the acme of Bhakti or Prema— supreme, pure and desireless devotion or love for God. But such Bhakti is very rare, it does not come of itself in the beginning. That is why the observance of Karma Kanda and of formal devotion has been enjoined by our scriptures. If these rites are observed with reverence and faith, the mind is gradually purified by the grace of God, its dross is washed away, the desire for pretty results appears contemptible, and aversion is felt for the fleeting objects of the world. Then the heart yearns to gain the imperishable,

16

highest state. That state is called Supreme
Bhakti or Supreme Jnana.

*   *   *

261. *Vâk-siddhi*, or perfection of speech,
is attained and Divine power is manifested
by the practice of unbroken Brahmacharya
or continence, and of truth for twelve years.
The words of such a person never prove
false; whatever he says to anybody comes
true—be it a curse or a blessing. Anyone
whose welfare he wishes fares well. Whatever resolution arises in his pure mind is
fulfilled.

*   *   *

262. Those who want to realise God
should not give up truth under any circumstances; for them it is better even to
suffer, if they have to, a thousand miseries
and afflictions than to sacrifice truth. If
one is prepared to do so, and faces all these
cheerfully, only then can one realise God,
Who is Truth itself. To lose Truth is to
lose God Himself. The power of truth is
unfailing: Rama went to the forest to fulfil the truth of his father's vow; the five
Pandavas, the sons of King Pandu, wel-
comed banishment along with Draupadi

for the sake of truth; and for the same reason King Harishchandra lost everything and became a street beggar. The Puranas contain hundreds of instances of unfaltering devotion to truth, even at the sacrifice of life. Our Master, Sri Ramakrishna, after the realisation of the Highest, offered to the Divine Mother Kali everything—both knowledge and ignorance, holiness and unholiness, good and evil, righteousness and unrighteousness, praying Her to take both pairs of opposites and give him pure Love. But he could not bring himself to say, "Mother, here is Thy Truth and here is Thy falsehood!" For, as he said, what would he hold on to, if he gave up Truth?

*   *   *

263. Time is fleeting like the wind. Life is on the wane every moment. Life is but another name of death. There is no knowing when this body will drop off. So you should always be prepared for the call of death. Do not waste your time in vain, do not put off any indispensable duty for some future time. Even from this very moment you should try to accumulate

something for the future life. Riches and property are resources for this world alone; they will not accompany you after your death. Spiritual practices and prayer are the resources for the hereafter. They are really your own possession which you can take along with you. However little that provision may be, nothing of it will be in vain; with its help you will have advanced that much further along the Way.

*   *   *

264. In the next life you will start with what you have acquired by practising spiritual disciplines in this life; that is to say, in the next life you will start exactly from where you leave off your spiritual practices in this life, and advance towards your Goal with rapid strides. It is for this reason that some persons are seen to be devoted to God by nature; by a little spiritual practice they gain one-pointedness of mind and intuitive experience of subtle truths; they just need a little stirring up to bring out their inner fire. *Diksha*, or initiation by the Guru, is this stirring up. Sri Ramakrishna used to call those souls 'dry fuel', who would blaze up into

a flame by a little blowing. The others he called 'wet or green wood' which does not burn easily, for whom the Guru has to undergo a lot of trouble. The Guru may blow and blow—but still they hardly show any sign of being kindled or roused into action. These persons themselves, even if they try, have also to toil long and hard. Many lives may perhaps pass away before they are able to attain Realisation of the Highest.

* * *

265. Everybody has to suffer the consequences of his past actions; there can be no liberation before the fruits of one's actions have been reaped, that is, before one has exhausted his experience of pleasure and pain, and learnt his lesson thereby. But if one takes refuge in an Incarnation of God, or some ever-perfect soul with special commission from God, then through the grace of such a one, the potential fruit-bearing tendencies which would have taken several lives to be worked out, are exhausted in this one life itself.

* * *

266. It is usually seen in the world that

those who walk along the path of righteousness have no end of worldly miseries
and suffering, and that many of those
who lead the life of unrighteousness and
have recourse to vice, seem to pass their
lives quite happily and in comfort. Because
the desire for the enjoyment of sense-
pleasures is very strong in these, it is
the be-all and end-all of their existence.
If they can secure objects of enjoyment by
any means whatsoever, they consider themselves very shrewd and think they are quite
happy. The worm that lives in filth finds
happiness in filth alone, and is nourished
by that also. But such people are so foolish
and deluded that they never reflect, that
they will have to endure terrible pain and
anguish in the next life for the burden of
misdeeds which they are accumulating in
this one. Who knows, because of their
bestial nature, they may even have to
transmigrate into a lower animal body!
Leaving that out of account, those who
are sunk in such profound ignorance,
those who do not feel stung by the
scorpion of conscience, are simply beasts in

human form.

* * *

267. Never for a moment suppose that those who are blinded by self-interest, who are slaves to their senses, or mad with the wine of ill-gotten riches, have real happiness and peace in their hearts, however smart and cheerful they may appear outwardly. Enjoyment of worldly objects seems sweet while it lasts, but there comes a time when it becomes the source of pain and troubles which gnaw the heart. The life of the self-indulgent becomes laden with constant fear, anxiety, uneasiness and ultimate frustration; they even go so far as to desire death or commit suicide. They are indeed objects of pity.

* * *

268. The mind is purified by good and noble thoughts, holy company and good deeds. Then only does it become quiet and become one-pointed in Japa and meditation. As the reflection in a dirty mirror is not clear, so, if the mind is impure, it is not able to grasp divine thoughts and ideas. For this reason, spiritual practices and prayers are essentially necessary. In the beginning

one has to force oneself to do these, even if the mind be disinclined for them. As you go on practising, you will find that you are developing a taste for them, and you will like them. If the patient does not want to take medicine, he has to be persuaded or forced to take it. But there are such patients also who spit out the medicine, even when it is put into their mouths. Then how can their disease be cured?

*　　　*　　　*

269. The more you go on performing your spiritual practices and austerities, the more you will feel the grace of God upon you, and His Presence in your heart. You will find how He is helping you in various ways; how, keeping Himself in the background, as it were, He is providing whatever is necessary for you to realise Him. Can the mind ever tend towards Him if He does not draw it? He instills such inspiration into the heart of one who ardently wants Him alone, who renounces everything for His sake, whose soul yearns to realise Him and does not find satisfaction in anything else. That divine discontent is called "the state of being mad with

Love". Intense yearning for God is, in essence, to live in Him. Yearning is the key to the inner portal of the Lord's mansion.

*   *   *

270. Do not think after doing Japa and meditation for some time: "Why, I have practised so much all these days, yet nothing at all has been gained!" If you do not get any result even after carrying on for a long time, know that there is in you some defect somewhere, that there is some crack or hole through which all your act of worship is leaking out, as water from a jar. Find that out by searching inside yourself and close it. Then only will your 'jar' gradually fill up, and the heart will be full of spiritual strength and bliss. "I am toiling so much, I am doing so much religious exercise"— it is delusion to have such ideas and a sign of egotism. Rather think: "However much I may try and toil, what an insignificant trifle it is towards realising Thee, O Lord? What capacity have I by virtue of which I can find Thee? If Thou showest me favour, out of Thy own mercy, then only can I find Thee. I have no other way.

I have taken refuge in Thee alone. Be Thou compassionate towards me out of Thy infinite mercy. Save me, O Lord, and deliver me from the bondage of existence!"

* * *

271. Meditation and Japa can be practised at all times, at all places, and in all conditions. Persons who have perfected themselves in meditation can, by drawing their minds within themselves, feel such solitude even amidst the din and uproar of the market place, that nothing can interrupt their one-pointedness. They remain the same in happiness and misery, in prosperity and adversity, in praise and blame. It is they who have been called in the Gita —Sthitadhi or persons of steady wisdom and knowers of Brahman.

* * *

272. In the same way, Japa is spontaneously done along with each breath (inhaling and exhaling) by those who have reached perfection in it; they do not have to make an effort to do that. It is that which is called Ajapâ Japa, or spontaneous repetition of the Mantra. These persons

attain such a state, in consequence of their
minds being firmly fixed on Japa by virtue
of repeated practice, that even though
they may remain occupied outwardly with
conversation or some work, the Mantra,
or the mystical formula of the Chosen
Ideal, continues constantly to be sounded
within them. If they feel so inclined they
also use a rosary for Japa when engaged
in talk or business for the teaching of men.
But it is not like telling beads with a
rattling noise for parading their religiosity,
as humbugs and the so-called Vaishnavas
do, while bargaining for vegetables and
other commodities! The stage reached by
a great soul, whether perfected by Dhyana
or by Japa, is the same. Both are the final
result of intense practice, control of mind,
spiritual effort and prayer over a long
period. "Mukti is in his possession who is
perfect in Dhyana."

*   *   *

273. Pranayama is the act of breathing
evenly and gently according to a special
process, that is, controlling the Prana, or
vital breath. If Pranayama is practised

methodically and properly over a long period, the mind becomes calm; it gets concentrated on the object to which it is applied, and perfect knowledge concerning that object is gained. This is pre-eminently the spiritual result of Pranayama. Its effect on the body and mind is also wonderful. It makes the body healthy, strong and radiant. The mind also becomes cheerful, calm and patient, virile and resolute; and irresistible will power and personal magnetism are manifest. So, whatever task the mind is applied to is accomplished. As a result of Pranayama, the Yogis reach long life and acquire many supernatural powers. But such powers are great hindrances to the realisation of the Supreme End.

*　　　*　　　*

274. It is seen in the world that the more slowly animals breathe, the longer lives they have; and those which breathe in quick succession are short-lived. In olden times the usual span of human life is said to have been a hundred years, because men lived in harmony with nature. According to the Vedas, "The span of human life is a hundred years".

According to the Svarodaya Yoga Shastra:

Species		Respiration per minute	Lifetime
Man (in ancient times)		12-13 times*	100 years
Elephant	..	11-12 „	100 „
Snake	..	7-8 „	120 „
Tortoise	..	4-5 „	150-155 „
Monkey	..	31-32 „	20-21 „
Hare	..	38-39 „	8

*   *   *

275. It is forbidden to breathe out with force. One should breathe out, according to the Yoga Shastras, with so little force that it would not blow away even *chhâtu* (barleymeal, or barley fried and then ground fine) placed in the palm of one's hand.

*   *   *

276. Those who try to empty the mind of all its content, or thought, right from the start of their Sadhana, without proper Shastric instructions, training and spiritual practices, and who think they are practising to attain the high state of seedless or Nirvikalpa Samadhi—total absorption in Pure Consciousness—by making the mind completely void of anything to hold on to,

---

* Nowadays it is generally 15-16 times, hence man is short-lived.

only bring themselves down to a Tamasic state; that is to say, they make themselves inert and imbecile. Their brain becomes blank, and hence they are incapable of grasping subtle truths.

* * *

277. According to the Siva Samhita, the first condition of success in Yoga is the belief, "I shall surely be successful". The second is, spiritual practice with faith and devotion; the third, worship of the Guru; the fourth, equanimity; the fifth, control of the senses; and the sixth, moderate eating. There is no seventh. That is to say, if these six conditions are properly fulfilled, nothing else is necessary, for success is inevitable. This applies without exception to all aspirants after liberation.

* * *

278. There is no other task in the world which is so difficult as the control of the mind. Sri Ramachandra said to Hanumâna: "One may cross the seven seas by swimming, suck in all the air, and play at ball with the mountain; but it is more difficult than all of these to control a restless mind." There is however no reason to

fear or to grow despondent even if this be so. The heroic aspirant can accomplish the impossible through the grace of God, if he struggles and performs spiritual practices, heart and soul, with infinite perseverance and firm resolution, relying on Him.

*   *   *

279. Swami Vivekananda composed a Sanskrit poem and sent it in a letter from America to his brother-disciples of the Math, of which two stanzas are given below:

"We shall chew up the stars, and
   uproot the three worlds by force.
Do you not know us? We are the
   servants of Sri Ramakrishna!"

Even the impossible is made possible by such tremendous self-confidence and devotion to the Guru. Because Swamiji had these, he conquered the world. Jesus has also said: "If ye have faith as a grain of mustard seed, ye shall say unto this mountain, remove hence to yonder place; and it shall remove; and nothing shall be impossible unto you." After the various spiritual experiences and visions of God which our Great Master Sri Ramakrishna

had, he said to the Mother, for verification:
"Mother, if all these divine experiences of
mine be true, this large boulder here will
jump up thrice." This happened, we are
told, as soon as he said it. Are these things
mere empty words?

*   *   *

280. Do the six lotuses really exist in the
body? When asked about it, Swamiji
replied: "Our Master used to say that the
lotuses described by the Yogis do not really
exist in the human body in material form,
but they come into existence and are perceived by them through the agency of the
power of Yoga."

*   *   *

281. Work is of three kinds according
to the distinction between the three Gunas,
Sattva, Rajas and Tamas. Good or beneficial work is Sattvic; bad or injurious,
Tamasic; and a mixture of these two,
Rajasic. The mark or the impress that is
left on the mind-stuff or on the subtle
body by actions, etc. is called Samaskâra.
That is what we call Karma, Adrishta—
the unseen (fate, destiny), Dharma and
Adharma (merit and demerit), Pâpa-

Punya (virtue and vice), etc. There can be no effect without cause. Our good or bad tastes or tendencies, whatever they may be, are all stimulations of Samskaras accumulated in the past. Only those among them which find favourable circumstances manifest themselves and become active. The others remain stored up, waiting for a suitable occasion, and bear good or bad results at the opportune moment. Whatever we do is a mixture of good and evil, hence we reap fruits in which both happiness and misery are mingled. We term a thing good or bad according as the one or the other predominates in it.

*   *   *

282. All work without exception causes bondage. Be it happiness or misery, each is bondage. There can be no Mukti until one goes beyond these two. Work never becomes a cause of bondage for those who work for the sake of others without the idea of "I", because they do not desire results, do not work to gain selfish ends, or for name and fame. Love springs in their hearts; seeing God in all beings, they work in the spirit of Service done to Him.

Consequently, their work consumes the potential results of all their accumulated action, and does not produce further seeds of any action in the form of fresh Samskaras in the mind. So, freed from the cause of repeated birth and death, they become fit for the attainment of Moksha, or liberation, after the dissolution of the body.

*   *   *

283. There is no happiness in sense enjoyment. In renunciation alone is true happiness. That person alone is supremely happy and inherits Immortality, who learns his lesson either by discrimination between the Real and the unreal or by repeated bitter experiences, who renounces everything of his own will, having lost all desire for the enjoyment of worldly objects, knowing them to be unsubstantial and ultimately pain-bearing. Swamiji has shown in his book *Bhakti Yoga* that renunciation is the very life and soul of all the four kinds of Yoga.

*   *   *

284. The Karma-Yogin dedicates the fruit of his work to God without being attached to it, since he knows that "God

alone is the doer, I am not the doer of action." The Raja-Yogin knows that "Prakriti, Nature, is for Purusha, the Self, and not Purusha for Prakriti." Purusha is the Atman, Self, Prakriti is Matter; so He is wholly different from Prakriti; their relation is temporary, that is, not eternal. Purusha is not subject to Prakriti. He is the master, Prakriti, the servant. Prakriti exists only for the accomplishment of His purpose. Her function is to take Him through various experiences and thereby make Him realise His own true nature. So the Raja-Yogin does not identify himself with Prakriti, and hence gives up all delusive attachment to her.

*   *   *

285. The renunciation of the Jnana-Yogin is the most difficult, because he has to assume right from the start that the whole universe and his relation to it are unreal—Maya—that the whole of life is like a dream. His path is: "*Neti, Neti*, not this, not this; I am not this nor that—nothing whatever I see or possess; I am neither body, nor mind, nor the senses; I have no pleasure, no pain, no birth, no death; I

have no bondage, no liberation; I am the Absolute Brahman, the Supreme Self; I am of the nature of Consciousness, Ever-pure, Ever-enlightened, Ever-free." Consciously he has to plunge into meditation on his own real essence, the Self, rejecting all external objects.

*　　　*　　　*

286. The renunciation of the Bhakti-Yogin is the easiest of all; it comes naturally. There is no hardship or auster-ity in it, no vain effort to suppress the mind by force; only, the tendencies of the mind have to be given a new direction; the course of their current has just to be turned into a new channel. When after experiencing constant misery, sorrow and despair, as a result of being attached to various kinds of worldly objects, a person realises their unsubstantial nature and turns away from desires, then his attachment to them slips away automatically, his heart and soul yearn to realise God who is Ever-true and Eternal, who is the perennial Source of Supreme Happiness; and Love and Devotion fill his heart. Sri Ramakrishna has therefore declared the

path of Bhakti to be the best suited to this
Kali-yuga, the iron age—the age of sin and
degradation.

*   *   *

287. He in whose life there is a perfect
harmony of Karma, Yoga, Jnana, and
Bhakti is the ideal Mahâpurusha, the greatest of saints, the world-teacher. The Divine
Master Śri Ramakrishna has given this new
ideal of Universal Religion to the world
after having practised it himself. It is the
Yuga-dharma, the Religion for this age.

*   *   *

288. As any of the four Yogas is impossible without Tyâga, or renunciation, even
so is true Bhoga, or enjoyment of worldly
objects, impossible without renunciation.
Enjoyment without renunciation is all
suffering, its only consequence is misery.
Men run away out of fear as soon as they
hear the word renunciation, because they
cannot conceive how much happiness there
is in it. If a person is called upon to renounce, why should it necessarily mean that
he must have to be a monk, giving up his
wife and children, his dear ones, hearth
and home, riches and property? Why not

practise a little renunciation of small things in daily life according to your capacity? Then you will understand how much happiness and joy there is in renunciation, how much it broadens the heart and cheers the mind. The renunciation which does not bring forth joy is no renunciation at all. It is something else.

*　　　*　　　*

289. Renunciation is, verily, the life of our life. We are, in fact, renouncing every moment without being aware of it. We are renouncing breath, that is to say, breathing in for breathing out, for the maintenance of our life; as blood collects in the heart through eating and other nourishment, so also at the same time it flows out into arteries and veins in order to invigorate them—otherwise death is inevitable. Whatever we receive from others or from nature, and whatever we earn —learning, knowledge of sciences, truths about the universe, riches and spirituality—is for the good of others, is for removing the want of others. If we grudge giving or distributing to others without stint, what we have wastes away

in course of time, and is of no use to anybody. Mark you, distribution—not exchange! A gift or an act of renunciation must be free, spontaneous, and bereft of any ulterior motive. Then only does it become productive of imperishable good. Swamiji has said, "Give, give away, do not seek return. Whoever seeks return, his ocean dwindles to a mere drop!"

* * *

290. The evidence of renunciation is seen everywhere in external nature. The sun, the moon, the stars are giving light and heat; trees are bearing fruits, giving shade and sending forth flowers, honey and fragrance; rivers are slaking thirst, and the earth is producing food and materials for the enjoyment of all living beings. All are giving themselves away freely, silently and according to their own nature, for the good of other beings. It is only man who makes himself wretched and ridiculous, crying even as he dies, "Mine! Mine!"

* * *

291. The Yogins and men of renunciation do not accept gifts from anyone for their own enjoyment, because that under-

mines their freedom and purity of mind. Acceptance of gifts begets a sense of obligation, and the sin of the donor defiles the body and the mind of the recipient. "Let me have this and that! Let this or that happen. I want this, I want that"—to be subject to desires like these and to accept gifts for their fulfilment, is called *Parigraha*. *Aparigraha*, or non-acceptance of gifts, is the attitude of desireless renunciation. But to accept something only for the upkeep of the body is not *Parigraha*. Then again, the Jnanis do not become attached even to that little, vital bodily need or comfort. They know for certain that there is no happiness in Bhoga or enjoyment in any shape, and they have no craving for happiness either. But if those among them who engage themselves in some kind of humanitarian activity, accept gifts for the sake of executing that work more efficiently and extensively, there is no harm in doing it.

*   *   *

292. The name and the object denoted by the name are identical; God and His name are selfsame. As His forms, attributes and conceptions are innumerable,

so His names also are countless. The power of His name is irresistible and infinite. Whatever name appeals to you, go on repeating that. He will respond to it. All desired ends can be fulfilled and He can be realised by the repetition of His name alone. "By Japa Realisation is gained."

* * *

293. But the Highest Realisation cannot be attained without submitting oneself to the spiritual instructions handed down in succession from the line of Gurus. This is called *Guru-paramparâ*. A power flows along the line of spiritual teachers from Guru to disciple, and when a disciple becomes in time a Guru, then in turn to his disciples. Thus, due to the rigorous spiritual practices of the Gurus from time immemorial, the mystic power of the holy names of the particular deities worshipped, has been concentrated in the form of special "seed-mantras". This Mantra is the aspirant's hope and stay, and the living symbol of his Chosen Ideal. If that Mantra is constantly practised through Japa with one-pointedness of mind, its great power is perceived as a reality. But one should have

Diksha, or initiation, in the manner enjoined, from a qualified spiritual person of pure mind who has received the holy name from the traditional line of Gurus. Then, if one follows spiritual disciplines according to his Guru's instructions, with full reverence and faith in him, Realisation comes quickly to him.

* * *

294. As a person sleeping in a room with closed doors wakes up to respond, if anybody knocks calling his name, and opens the door, in the same way, if anyone takes the name of God repeating His holy Mantra, and performs spiritual practices with simple faith and zealous devotion, the Lord who dwells in all beings wakes up and opens the door of the temple of the aspirant's heart, to fulfil his cherished desire, and reveals Himself to him in the form of his Chosen Deity.

* * *

295. Such is the infinite glory and power of the name of God that by uttering it, the sinner, the afflicted, even the reviler find salvation; and the undevout comes to find a sweet taste in it and devel-

ops an aversion for worldly objects. If you are not able to do any other spiritual practice, at least go on repeating His name and pray to Him yearningly; you will then have strength and peace of mind, and in course of time will gain love and devotion for Him through His grace.

*   *   *

296. Tapasyâ, or asceticism, is of three kinds—of body, of speech and of mind. Practice of physical austerities, like vows and penances, and the service of the diseased and the afflicted, and such acts, are asceticism of the body. Truthfulness is asceticism of speech. Restraint of the senses and the practice of concentration on the object of meditation, is asceticism of the mind. He who seeks to gain the highest Realisation must practise these threefold Tapasya.

*   *   *

297. Religion in its essence means the desire for God and a feeling of want for Him. We keenly feel the need of such things only without which it is impossible to live, as for example, air, food, clothes and shelter. Do we really want God in the

same way? In fact, we want everything
else except Him, because all the ordinary
wants usually needed for our living are
satisfied by the external world itself. It is
only when we feel the acute need for
something that cannot be supplied by the
objective world, when we realise that it has
no power to quench the thirst and satisfy
the hunger of the heart, then only do we
turn our eyes within and seek for help
there. When after we have experienced
repeated suffering, the lesson is burnt into
us that all that we have been doing is
child's play, that the world is unreal like a
dream, that whatever we try to grasp as
our own slips out of our hands—then the
heart yearns for some everlasting object by
getting which all miseries and wants will
be annihilated root and branch. That object
is God alone. Such a trend of the mind is
the first step to religion, namely, aversion
for worldly objects and the feeling of a real
want for God.

*   *   *

298. *Shrimad Bhâgavata* gives the following lineage of Adharma or Irreligion as the
cause of perdition. The wife of Irreligion

is Falsehood. To them were born a son named Pride and a daughter named Maya (delusion). They married each other and had a son named Avarice and a daughter named Deceit. From the union of these two were born Anger and Envy. Kali (the Iron Age) is their son and Evil-Speech is their daughter. Kali raised from Evil-Speech a daughter called Fear and a son called Death. Torment and Hell are their issue, and of none else.

* * *

299. And the family of Dharma or Religion, the cause of the attainment of the Four Supreme Values of human life, is stated therein to consist of thirteen sisters, as follows:—Faith, Amity, Compassion, Peace, Contentment, Nourishment, Activity, Progress, Intelligence, Strength, Forbearance, Modesty and Murti (Form). These are the thirteen wives of Religion. Among them, Faith gave birth to a son named Truth, Amity to Serenity, Compassion to Fearlessness, Peace to Self-restraint, Contentment to Delight, Nourishment to Dignity, Activity to Yoga, Progress to Self-respect, Intelligence to Wealth, Strength

to Memory, Forbearance to Well-being, and Modesty to Humility. And Murti (Form), the youngest wife of Religion, the source of all virtues, gave birth to the Godlike Rishis Nara and Nârâyana—the Man-God and the God-Man.

        *   *   *

300. In the case of a conflict between the head and the heart, listen always to the voice of the heart. The head is the chief centre of the intellectual faculties, of the organs of knowledge or perception which are (1) the ear, of hearing; (2) the eye, of sight; (3) the nose, of smell; (4) the skin, of touch; and (5) the tongue, of taste. From the head alone we get all the requisite mental power to acquire the knowledge of any object. The heart is the seat of all feelings, impulses and experiences touching the core of personality. Men of intellect acquire proficiency in the various scriptures and branches of learning and sciences. They are pre-eminently learned scholars and teachers, of sharp intelligence, skilful and expert in various things. Men of heart are richly endowed with noble qualities like compassion, breadth of mind,

sympathy for the suffering of others, love for all beings, etc. The heart alone inspires man with the highest sentiments and leads him into the realm of Self-Realisation, forbidden to intellect and reason. A man of book-learning can be selfish, cruel and villainous, but a large-hearted person can never be of that nature even at the cost of his life.

* * *

301. Cultivate the heart in as many ways as you can. The heart is the *Gomukhi*, the primal source, of the Gangâ of Love. It is through the heart alone that the Voice of God is heard; it is in the cave of the heart alone that He reveals Himself. There is no need studying the scriptures, or acquiring learning, in order to find Him and to attain Jnana, Bhakti and Moksha. Character is not formed nor personality developed by reading books—they only make learned fools. "Not Grantha (book), but Granthi (knot, i.e. bondage)"—Sri Ramakrishna used to say.

* * *

302. The modern mode of learning, in particular, is a veritable hotchpotch of in-

compatibles; it brings about mental in-
digestion in many instances. It is not
'passing' (an examination), but passing
a '*pâsh*' (rope) round the neck. But alas,
what an infatuation for 'passing' has taken
hold of us, Indians! We devote to it
the whole of our mental and physical
energy in youth, the best time of life. In
spite of poverty we collect money for this
purpose with great difficulty, endure so
much physical pain and mental worry—
and what return do we usually get in
the long run? Loss of health and seeing
darkness everywhere, because of defeat in
the struggle for existence! And to crown
all, if over and above this, one has to
maintain wife and children as a result of
early marriage, what a fine mess one finds
himself in! It is not without truth that
our universities have been called 'slave-
barracks', or factories for the manufacture
of slaves. School or college education, as
it has turned out, is neither bread-win-
ning nor of much use in practical life;
rather it is harmful and soul-killing. It is
especially among the so-called 'educated'
that a large proportion is found to be

without moral backbone, without faith in religion, denationalised and living-dead. Only those who are endowed with unusually good Samskaras manage to survive.

* * *

303. Having been born in this rare human life, try to find Him, by finding Whom everything is obtained and nothing else remains to be gained. Strive to know Him, by knowing Whom everything becomes known and nothing else remains to be known. Love Him, by loving Whom all other objects of love—all attachment to 'Woman and Gold'—appear to be but dust and ashes. Build up your life in such a way that you may attain deathless life.

* * *

304. But then one must have that kind of urge and devotion to the highest Ideal. Spiritual practice is wanted—single-minded rigorous practice. An ounce of practice weighs more than a ton of profession. A drop of Prema or Divine Love slakes thirst better than scriptural knowledge as vast as the ocean. Prema is, as it were, thickened-milk, cream or butter; and all learning, as of the Vedas and other sacred scriptures,

is, as it were, butter-milk. Discussions on doctrines, learned elucidation of the Shastras, or sacred scriptures, lectures and such like, are for men of a lower level—let them be happy with those things. Let those who want, drink butter-milk; but you take thickened-milk, cream and butter to your heart's content.

*   *   *

305. Purity is like Mount Kailâs capped by the eternal snows, the abode of the True, the Good and the Beautiful. The Lord is reflected only in the pure heart. The great spiritual truths unfold themselves only in a pure soul. Ages ago, our Yogis and Rishis discovered prodigious truths about the atom, about the five subtle and primary elements, about the internal workings of the body—that is, the activities going on inside the body in its threefold aggregate of the gross body, the organic or subtle body and the elemental body, and the diseases that occur if their activities deviate from their normal functions—about the courses and influence of the stars, physics, astrology etc., which are corroborated by modern science. How

was it possible? They never had scientific instruments like the telescope or the microscope, nor laboratories with all the modern equipment. The abstruse truths which they discovered or which were revealed to them, simply by intently focussing the inward vision of their pure minds on the problems at issue, are a wonder to the savants of the civilised world of today.

306. If you long to have the Supreme Love of God, Jnana and Moksha, you must become pure within and without. Both the body and the mind must be cleansed and pure. The means to this, the Master used to say, is "renunciation of Woman and Gold," that is, lust and possessions. Such renunciation is extremely difficult but not impossible. Struggle with all your heart and soul. Continuous practice— intense self-effort and spiritual discipline— makes everything possible. But it is not even possible to make this self-effort without the Grace of God. It is true that "Only one or two in a million are cut free (as in kite-flying)". But who can say

that you will not be one of those "one or two"? So go ahead with this faith in you.

*   *   *

307. We are conscious sinners. We do not refrain from committing sin even knowing what we are doing, and even though it brings about suffering; and yet we shed crocodile tears over it, pretending to be foolish, ignorant or stupid. Those who sin deliberately are indeed atheists. Sinners as such have a chance of salvation, but there is no liberation for wilful sinners. Who can wake up one who only feigns to be sleeping? Religion is not a child's play! Nothing at all worth having can be gained until "the mind and the mouth"—words and actions—are harmonised, unless one is sincere to the core.

*   *   *

308. No great work is accomplished by cunning or deception. You can impose upon people by outward show and high-sounding phrases; but hypocrisy will be of no avail with regard to God. You will only deceive yourself. All your spiritual practices and prayers will be mere fruitless labour like pouring water into a leaky jar.

Great work is done and character is formed only by indefatigable toil and complete self-sacrifice.

*   *   *

309. "I shall do nothing," "I cannot do anything," "It can be carried through only if you do it for me"—these are the words of imbeciles. "Lift up to my mouth, I shall eat then!" It is better both for society and for the persons themselves who have this sort of attitude that they should die; and, by the law of nature, they do die, losing strength and vitality slowly and steadily. To live in constant expectation of help from others, or from some outward agency, visible or invisible, is as good as death. Freedom is heaven, dependence on others is hell.

*   *   *

310. Why should one have to be a fatalist if one accepts the doctrine of Karma? The law of Karma has eternally proclaimed the message of Freedom to man. If I have got myself bound and have degraded myself by my bad Karma, then it stands to reason that I shall surely be able to lift myself up through the influence of my

good Karma. If I can bind myself, then I can certainly untie that bond also. The difference is only between will and action. Why should we not be able to free ourselves by cutting the bonds of bad Karma with right resolution, good deeds and righteous mode of living? Humanity would have gone stark mad if there had been no possibility of ever attaining Liberation. Then again, why should we proceed to do good work at all or strive to be spiritual by sacrificing ourselves, if we can profit more or further our interest by misdeeds? Had it been so, all spirituality, goodness, compassion and all love and fellow-feeling would have vanished from the world and men would have turned themselves into veritable beasts.

*   *   *

311. How can God, who is Infinite, incarnate Himself in the small, limited human frame? To this question Swamiji replied: "Yes, it is true that God is Infinite, but not in the way you conceive it. You understand 'Infinite' according to your gross ideas, as a vast material object which fills the whole universe. That is

why you wonder how so large and vast an
entity like God can contract itself to enter
this tiny little human body. In truth, by
'Infinity of God' is meant only His un-
limited spiritual Essence, and hence, that
is not restricted in the least by His incar-
nating Himself in a human body."

*   *   *

312. He who is Brahman-without-attri-
butes is Himself Brahman-with-attributes.
There is no difference between the Brahman
with attributes and an Avatâra or Incarnation of God. But there is difference
between an Avatara and a Jiva, or individual soul. Man is compelled to take birth
again and again under the influence of his
own actions; but an Incarnation assumes
human form in every age, out of His divine
free-will, for the preservation of the world,
for the destruction of irreligion, and for the
resuscitation of religion, and also to confer
His grace upon holy men and devotees.
Furthermore, the Jivas are born subject to
Prakriti or Nature, which is constituted
by the three Principles—Sattva, Rajas and
Tamas. But an Avatâra is not subject to
Prakriti nor to the three Principles—He is

their Master and Controller. The Avatâra is God made manifest—only the external shell of human form is material.

       *   *   *

313. All that we can conceive of as the highest and most glorious of attributes, we find manifested and can realise fully, only in an Avatara. He is the concrete embodiment of all Divine attributes. God Himself plays in multifarious ways in the human body which He assumes. But the Avatara reveals His own nature only to a limited number of pure-hearted devotees and closest associates for the purpose of accomplishing His special mission in the world. Since He behaves exactly like a human being, ordinary people fail to grasp and recognise Him, and even ridicule Him during His lifetime.

       *   *   *

314. How can self-effort and mercy of God be harmonised? These two appear to be contradictory, but it is not so. Self-effort is also a gift of God, His mercy. Devotees without manliness are of a lower class. See how virile and heroic were the devotees, Mahâvira, Arjuna and Prahlâda!

Hanumâna (Mahâvira) had no fear even of crossing the sea; he crossed it in one bound shouting "Victory to Rama"! Prahlâda did not quail even when repeatedly faced with death, but took refuge in Vishnu with his mind merged in Him. As a result, He appeared and saved him. Arjuna's prowess is universally known. There are many hundreds of other shining examples in the Puranas.

* * *

315. The heroic devotee says: "What should I be afraid of, being a child of the Mother, being a servant of God? What is there that I cannot do?" The heroic devotee exclaims:

"Whom do I fear in this world
Whose Queen is the Mother, the
Goddess Supreme?..
I can buy the estate of Brahmamayee
(the Mother who is Brahman) with
the strength of my devotion."

Thus again:

"Come Thou, Mother, to this field of
spiritual battle! Let me see who gets
defeated, Mother or son."
"Today, O Mother, I shall settle this

once for all by fighting Thee; what
       fear is there in death?
I shall easily capture the treasure of
       Mukti by sound of drum, as it were.
The twang of my tongue booms vibrant
       the name of Kali,
Who dares tarry on in battle with me?
The Sâdhaka Rasikchandra says: O
       Mother, mine!
I shall conquer Thee in battle by virtue
       of Thine own strength!"

The Master used to call this appropriately,
"robber-like Bhakti"; that is to say, Bhakti
by violence, swooping down on the Mother's
treasure store of jewels and plundering it
with the terrific war-cry of "Mâr, Mâr!"*

    *   *   *

316. God helps and becomes compassionate to those who have manliness.
Devotees without courage, enthusiasm and
zeal are sterile, lifeless, and hence Tamasika
by nature. They think: "We take God's
name morning and evening and find some
joy. He will show His mercy and take us
to the Goal when the time for it comes.

---

* Lit. Kill and destroy! Down with all opposition!

Whatever we get now is enough." Yearning to realise God comes to them only after many births. These are like petty house-breaking burglars, full of fear, and satisfied with whatever little they may lay their hands upon. And yet they too must be expert thieves, for, after all, it is theft in a house in which the owner is wide awake!

*   *   *

317. Swamiji could not bear a wretched, demeaning attitude in anyone. He hated it. He used to say, "That is atheism; that is a sort of disease, a dementia. If one goes on decrying oneself, thinking, 'I am nothing, I am good-for-nothing,' one becomes a non-entity. Is saying that humility or concealed egoism? 'I am a sinner. I am wholly worthless, I am weak'—by continuing to think so, one becomes all the more so. 'The Self cannot be realised by the weak!' Those who are weak in body and mind cannot practise religion. It is not for them. No work of any worth whatever can be expected of them. Fling those cursed ideas to the winds. On the contrary, be positive and say: 'In truth I

have infinite strength within myself. That power must be roused.' He who regards himself as a lion, 'gets out of the meshes of the world like a lion breaking out of cage'. You must be a hero. 'Abhih, Abhih!' Fearless! Fearless! You must trample fear under foot—whether you practise religion or lead a worldly life. Otherwise, you will ever remain sunk 'in that darkness in which you are already!' "

* * *

318. Whatever is done for the real good of one's self and of others is religion. All the rest is irreligion.

* * *

319. However much you may give counsel and instruction to persons who have not felt the actual need for Self-realisation within, and do not have the thirst for Liberation, it is all in vain. They listen with one ear and it all goes out of the other. In our country, even the illiterate peasants and village-folk are philosophers. They instinctively understand the higher truths of religion better than many scholars of the West. "Brahman is true, and the world false"—we have been hearing this saying

since our very childhood. If the soil is not made ready and good seeds are not sown in proper time, how will the crop come up to expectation? The devotion of those whose taste for worldly pleasure has dried up, blazes up forthwith like a spark of fire falling on a pile of hay. Lâlâ Babu left his home, renouncing the world, hearing just one word of the washerman: "Set fire to Vasana!"* Vilvamangal was roused to his senses by the rebuke of a harlot. He at once renounced the world and became a beggar for the love of Krishna. What a wonderful and austere life of devotion they led in Vrindaban and reached their cherished Goal! It comes exactly in like manner to those who are to attain Realisation in this very life.

*   *   *

320. Be perfectly sincere, and all your sins will be forgiven. Sincerity will save you from a multitude of sins. A man of sincerity, even though he be an abject

---

* There is a pun on the word Vasana here, which in Bengali means both desire and dried stalks of plantain trees, which are burnt into ashes by washermen for alkali to clean clothes.

sinner, wins the grace of God in time and becomes saintly.

* * *

321. Life is not a barren soil. Without proper care and cultivation, it becomes a jungle full of wild plants and wild beasts, creeping snakes and scorpions, thus always giving rise to fear. If this very soil—this life of man—is carefully cultivated, if the spiritual disciplines enjoined by the Guru are strenuously practised with faith and devotion, it will bring forth priceless wealth of happiness, peace and blessedness. Thus sang Sadhaka Ramprasada:

"O my mind, thou dost not know
the art of cultivation.
Such good soil—this human life—
is left fallow;
It would have yielded thee gold
and diamonds."

* * *

322. There is nothing in the world which is dull, dead matter. That which we call so, is nothing but consciousness or intelligence covered over by *tamas*, darkness or Ignorance. When that covering of *tamas* is removed, the darkness of Maya

will vanish, and the pure consciousness or the Supreme Spirit will be revealed. The world will then appear to be all-Spirit, and the fountain of Bliss will be overflowing.

*　　　*　　　*

323. In the universe, no action, no thought, no energy is lost. At some time or other, in some unthought-of-way, it will bear fruit either in your life or someone else's here or hereafter, in the shape of happiness or misery, according to the nature of the impulse, good or bad. So, you of noble intentions, if you desire the highest good, follow the path of righteousness and shun the path of evil.

*　　　*　　　*

324. Sree Sree Chandi is a portion of the Mârkandeya Purana, and is the most holy book of the worshippers of the *Shakti* cult. It is chanted with due Shâstric ceremonies and injunctions, either daily or on special lunar days, in solemn rites for propitiating inauspicious planets or deities, to avert impending or possible evil, to secure prosperity, or to get rid of some incurable disease, and invariably as an adjunct of the Puja of the Divine Mother. Swamiji

used to say that such a perfect and all-embracing idea of the Supreme Godhead as is depicted in the Chandi, in the meditation and worship of the Devi or Divine Mother, cannot be found in any other religious scripture of the world. Moreover, there are many things to be learnt and practised from the Chandi. One of them is—to look upon *all* women as mother, as part of the Mother of the Universe, and they should be respected as such. This attitude we find uniquely illustrated in the life of Sri Ramakrishna.

*   *   *

325. The Chandi describes how, in the battle between the Devas and the Asuras, or demons, Devi Chandikâ sprang up as bodying forth the combined power of all the Devas, and how by this personified embodiment of the aggregate energy of the Devas, the terrific force of the innumerable dreadful demons was defeated. Shakti-worship is, in fact, invocation of the concentrated Divine Power in the form of the Mother of the Universe.

*   *   *

326. Applying the above lesson to our

present situation in India: If for the purpose of doing good to our country and to our people, we forget all distinctions among ourselves and our personal self-interest, and unite and work together with one mind under a chosen leader obeying him implicitly—then any hostile power, however mighty it may be, cannot, dare not, stand against us or subdue us. We shall be victorious on all fronts.

*   *   *

327. In so far as we Hindus are not a compact organised community, we have become weak and helpless. Hence we are tyrannised over in various ways, and have to bear everything silently, and making a virtue of necessity we console our minds with the idea that we are practising Ahimsa, but in fact we are deceiving ourselves. Mahatma Gandhi condemned this as the non-violence of the weak. Observance of real Ahimsa, according to him, is the non-violence of the strong, that is, cherishing the spirit of Ahimsa towards your enemy and treating him with love, in spite of your full power and ability to retaliate against his acts of tyranny and

19

crush him. This was also the view of
Swamiji. In order to avenge a wrong or
an outrage, said he, if you are unable to
give back slaps on both the cheeks of your
aggressor in return for one received, or if
seeing that he is ready to kill you, you
cannot kill him, then how can you claim
to be called a man? Such non-violence on
your part is no sign of manliness. This is
also the teaching of the Hindu scriptures.

* * *

328. Before Swamiji made his pilgrimage
to Amarnath, someone asked him, "Sir,
what should we do when we see the strong
oppress the weak?" He at once replied,
"Why, thrash the strong, of course!"
"Even forgiveness," he said on a similar
occasion, "if weak and passive, is not true!
Fight is better. *Forgive* when you could
bring legions of angels to an easy victory.
. . . " "For the householder, self-defence!"

* * *

329. Thus, for the Hindus, in order
to live as a nation, the acquisition of
strength is absolutely necessary. The principal means of attaining it is unity. If
we have a firm faith in our religion, if

we do not shrink from laying down our lives for the sake of religion, no one will dare to vilify our religion or desecrate our images and our temples. Nor could any one dare to violate our women and treat them in abominable and inhuman ways. There is no other way for the Hindus to survive as a nation except by uniting and being of one mind. For the sake of preserving Dharma, society, culture and themselves, if they can unite, forgetting class distinctions and the particular interests of self and group, doing away with malice and enmity among themselves, then the people of other faiths will be afraid of vilifying our religious usages or injunctions.

* * *

330. In the days of the Baranagore Math, Swamiji told his Gurubhais the following parable: A landlord had two gardeners. One of them used to sit most of the time before him with folded hands and speak in a voice choked with devotion: "Aha! How beautiful are the eyes of my master! What a charming nose! What a handsome appearance!" and so forth. The other gardener worked the

whole day long in the fields and produced
varieties of vegetables, fruits and flowers,
and placing them before his master every
day, saluted him bowing down before him
and went away. With which of the two was
the landlord more pleased? In the same
way, the Lord is more highly pleased with
him who performs his duties with his whole
body and mind, looking upon all work as
His worship, than with one who seeks to
propitiate Him only by singing hymns or
Hallelujahs, neglecting his duties. Address-
ing his Gurubhais, Swamiji exclaimed,
"Take care that you do not get mixed up
with the gang of 'How beautiful are thy
eyes! What a charming nose!' or with
Ghantânârâr Daley, that is, those who only
ring the bell before the Deity in vesper
service!"—meaning, those whose whole
occupation is ceremonial worship.

* * *

331. Attainment of spirituality means
Realisation of the Atman or Self. He who
has it is truly religious. As a matter of
fact, we are all atheists. If we could see
God within and outside ourselves, if we
were convinced that He is omnipresent,

how could we commit sinful actions? If we could believe that He, being omniscient, knows all the evil thoughts we are thinking, should we not have desisted from them in sheer shame? If we knew that He, being omnipotent, has the power of throwing us into hell as punishment for our sinful acts, would we not out of fear of Him desist from them? We try to be good outwardly because of shame, scandal or punishment—but not in the true sense. Posing as religious, we do not refrain from doing unrighteous acts, taking care only to do them ingeniously and secretly, avoiding the public eye, lest we be found out. Those who admit themselves as atheists are a thousand times better than people of such character.

*　　　*　　　*

332. Swamiji used to say: Help others whenever you can and all you can, but mind what your motive is. If it is done for some selfish end or for gaining some advantage, know it will neither specially benefit those you help, nor yourself. On the other hand, if your motive is unselfish, your service will bring not only happiness

and welfare to others but infinite blessings upon yourself. This is as certain as that you are living.

* * *

333. Puja or worship is of two kinds—external (ceremonial) and mental. In the former, Puja is performed before the image or the picture of the Deity, an earthen or metal jar, wood or stone symbol, etc. by invoking the life-breath in them. Since we are human beings, all those things are offered in worship which are necessary for maintaining life, or which give us pleasure, satisfaction or contentment. These are, for instance, water for washing the feet and mouth, *Arghya,* a seat, dress, decorations, garlands of flowers, ornaments, sweet-scented flowers, sandal-wood paste, incense, lighted lamps, *Naivedya,* fruits and roots, sweets, cooked rice, *puris* and *curries, pâyasa* or thickened milk-rice, drinking-water, *tâmbula* (betel-leaves prepared with spices for chewing after meals)—then, a bed, fanning, chanting of hymns, vocal and instrumental music, dancing, *Âratrika* or the vesper service of waving of lights and burning camphor, etc. Lacking any or all of

the above materials and accessories, Puja
can be done even with offering of water
only as their substitute, with Bhakti.

*   *   *

334. In mental worship, there is no need
of any materials or accessories or even
an image of the Deity. Meditating on
His form as residing in the heart, and
imagining that you are offering the above
objects of worship mentally to the Deity,
is called mental Puja. In this Puja, the
Brahmin, the *Chandâla*, and the so-called
"untouchable"—all have equal rights. In
this Puja, there is no obligation to observe
physical purity or ceremonial cleanliness,
time or place or any Shastric injunctions.
Only absorption of mind is required.

*   *   *

335. All food or eatables are the general
property of living beings, everyone has a
share in it—this is the teaching of the
Upanishads. One cannot put into his
mouth even a morsel of food without
depriving or causing harm or pain to
another. Without first offering the food
to the Deity and laying aside the share of
hungry *Atithis* or wandering supplicants,

and of beasts and birds, he who cooks food only for himself and eats it, is called a sinner in our Shastras and such food is said to be sinful. The Shastras even prescribe sufferings in hell for the householder who eats food without giving part of it to a hungry man. (*Brihadâranyaka Upanishad*, Chap. I, 5th Brâhmana, 2nd Sloka). According to one's capacity, one must do one's utmost.

* * *

336. Whatever is performed to gain happiness or some selfish end for oneself or for one's own family and relatives, is not Dharma, but merely a worldly affair. Love or attachment for one's wife, children and relatives is called Maya. It pertains to worldly life, or *Samsâra*. Love for all beings is *Prema, Dayâ*, or compassion. Similarly, whatever works of religious merit, such as austerities, worship or religious disciplines, are practised with the object of gaining happiness and welfare in this life or in the next, are selfish acts, and in that sense not Dharma, or spirituality. But the selfsame actions, executed for the good and happiness of all beings without any desire for

enjoyment of fruits, performed with the idea that all may be equal sharers in their merits, bring forth fruits a thousandfold both for oneself and others. Lord Buddha, the embodiment of mercy, declared, "Until all the individuals in the world attain salvation, I do not want my own Mukti!" What a grand ideal!

* * *

337. But if by doing work unselfishly for the good of others you secretly nourish the hope of obtaining a thousandfold result, then it is no more *Nishkâma Karma*, that is, work without desire. Rather it is the same as desiring the thousandfold fruit by doing onefold. This is just like the foolish people who are tempted by cheats to convert ten-rupee notes into those of one hundred-rupee denomination, or who hand over gold coins or ornaments to them to be changed into their hundredfold weight, and who ultimately lose everything in the bargain.

* * *

338.* As Sri Ramakrishna was the living

* The ten paragraphs from 338 to 347 are adapted from the "Udbodhan".

embodiment of the harmony of all religions, so also was he the shining example of the perfection in practice of the fourfold Yoga of Jnana, Bhakti, Karma and Raja-Yoga in conjunction. This is the only means of moulding a perfect all-round character. Illumined by the light of his life, Swamiji proclaimed this grand truth of simultaneous practice of the fourfold Yoga, and set it forth as the path of Sadhana and the ideal of the Ramakrishna Math and the Mission founded by him. This idea has been beautifully illustrated by him in the emblem of the Ramakrishna Math and the Mission, which is a creation of his genius. It is reproduced below, with the interpretation given by him.

*　　*　　*

339. The expanse of the waters of the lake in the form of the waves in the picture represents Karma, the lotus—Bhakti, and  the rising sun—Jnana. The serpent coiling round stands for the awakened Kula-Kundalini Power and the swan symbolizes the Paramatman, the Supreme Self.

Thus the emblem conveys the idea that when Yoga comes into union with Karma, Bhakti and Jnana, Paramatman is realised.

*   *   *

340. Realisation of the Atman does not mean only the perception of Brahman as one's self, but also seeing all beings as Brahman. According to the Upanishads, to see Brahman everywhere, within and without oneself, is the sign of Supreme Realisation or Mukti. We find direct evidence of this in the lives of Sri Chaitanya and Sri Ramakrishna. This doctrine of the identity of Jiva and Brahman, being the object of the Sadhana of the Yogis and Rishis living in the hills and forests and of a small number of spiritual aspirants, was so long hidden in mountain caves or confined within the pages of the Shastras and the scholarly discourses or discussions of the philosophers. Swamiji having received hints from Sri Ramakrishna as to how this great truth could be practically applied in the daily lives of householders and Sannyasins without distinction, proclaimed to the world his path of serving all beings by seeing Narayana in them. He insisted

that by practice the Vedantic doctrine of
the identity of Jiva and Brahman can be
directly perceived and applied to the service
of man. With the object of teaching mankind that the ideal of "one's own salvation
and doing good to the world", is not only
not self-contradictory but mutually helpful,
he established the Ramakrishna Math and
the Ramakrishna Mission.

*   *   *

341. The doctrine of the Service of
Nara-Narayana, or Man as God, initiated
by Swamiji is an entirely new thing. It
is radically different from the humanitarian
service performed by the Bhikshus of the
Buddhist period, or conducted by the
Roman Catholic monks of the Middle
Ages. The service of suffering humanity
performed by the Buddhist monks was
inspired by mercy and compassion, and as
a means of helping them in their attainment of Nirvana. Such service done by
the Catholic monks was also prompted by
mercy and compassion. But in such methods
of service, the idea of distinction between
Sevya-Sevaka, or the served and the server,
is unavoidable. Those who serve in this

way place themselves on a higher pedestal and hold it to be the duty of the served to be grateful to them. But service of the "afflicted Narayanas and the poor-Narayanas"—words coined by Swamiji—based on the idea of Advaita or oneness of the Upanishads, as proclaimed by him, makes no difference between the giver and the recipient, for they are one from the standpoint of the Atman. Besides that, because the recipients afford the Sevakas the opportunity as well as the right and privilege of serving them as Narayana, the latter should rather feel grateful to them. Swamiji has even said, "Let the giver kneel down and worship, let the receiver stand up and permit!" What a world of difference between the old and the new idea!

*　　*　　*

342. If the God or the Goddess can be invoked and worshipped as the Brahman or the indwelling Atman, in dull, dead matter, like an earthen or wooden image, an earthen or metal jar, a stone or a picture, then why cannot such worship be done to the living man—the greatest of God's Creations? Man-worship does not mean

worship of his gross body but the worship
of the Narayana who resides as the Atman
within him. To perceive that the same
Narayana who is the Atman within me, is
also within all men and women, that He
is before me in the form of the ignorant,
the poor and the diseased—to serve these
with the eye of non-difference, with all
care and devotion, giving them knowledge,
food, clothes and medicine, nursing them,
etc.—constitutes in letter and in spirit the
worship of man. As in the Puja of other
Gods and Goddesses, in this worship also,
unless there be the idea of non-difference
of the Atman, it all turns into wasted
labour. The Shastras also say, "Worship
Shiva by being Shiva yourself." "Worship
the Deva by being Deva yourself."

*　　　*　　　*

343. This Nara-Narayana worship insti-
tuted by Swamiji is not merely unselfish,
unattached Karma for the good of others
in order to gain purification of one's heart,
but it is entirely a new process of Sadhana
for the realisation of the Paramatman, or
the Highest Self, through the practice of
a wonderful harmony of Jnana, Yoga,

Bhakti and Karma. And because it is so, it directly leads to the attainment of Mukti. For in this path man has to conceive of God through Jnana-Yoga as one's own self, meditate on God through Raja-Yoga as the Self within, to be attached to Him through Bhakti-Yoga with whole-souled devotion, and through Karma-Yoga serve Him with disinterested, desireless actions.

* * *

344. This Nara-Narayana doctrine of Swamiji which assigns to man the highest honour, has a unique distinction apart from the fact that it is a means to Mukti. According to it, man is not low and depraved and an object of pity, but is Shiva, deserving of the highest respect. Most of the priests and preachers of religions, posing as the sole representatives of God on earth, have placed Him high in the heavens on a jewelled throne as the stern judge, dispensing eternal punishment in hell for the sins of men who are born in sin. And the keys of heaven being in the possession of the priests, the latter have promulgated it as the Divine Law that sinners and repentants will acquire the

right of entering into heaven only if they
can propitiate God's representatives on earth
by giving them money or valuable possessions.

*   *   *

345. Standing against this deadly doctrine,
Swami Vivekananda proclaimed in a thun-
derous voice before the World's Parliament
of Religions at Chicago: "Ye children of
immortal bliss, who says ye are sinners?
Ye are heirs of Immortality! It is a sin to
call you sinners! Knowing the Supreme
Lord, go across the ocean of birth and
death. There is no other path of liberation." What immortal message of hope!
From the viewpoint of the Atman, the
so-called lower classes, the helpless, the
indigent, the "untouchables", are the living
Shiva, and hence worthy of our service
and worship. This glad tidings was for the
first time delivered with words of authority
by Swami Vivekananda, and the shining
light of his inspiration was his divine Master,
Sri Ramakrishna.

*   *

346. In modern times, we find all the
world over that man is mercilessly killing

man, one nation is heartlessly bringing
about the destruction of another nation,
all for the satisfaction of their own selfish
interest. In this age man's indignity to
man—insult to Humanity—man's vile attitude to man, his domineering and ill-
bred behaviour, have gone to the extreme.
In blood-thirstiness, man has surpassed even
the wild, ferocious animals of the jungle.
The powerful, so-called advanced nations
of the East and the West, in the pious
name of patriotism and national progress,
and on the plea of establishing peace and
spreading civilisation, are bringing about
utter ruin to the weak and backward
nations by robbing them of all their wealth
and possessions. In the eyes of the West
the non-white, non-Christian peoples of
the East are not men, they are uncivilised
barbarians! Aye! They are created by God
as instruments for the production of objects
of enjoyment for His chosen people, the
white overlords! Such an offensive outlook, and the rivalry among themselves
for the ownership of all the materials of
enjoyment, were the root causes of the
two World Wars in our generation which

ended in universal cataclysm.

*   *   *

347. In India also, in the name of religion, society, sect and *Adhikâravâda*—or the doctrine of special rights and privileges in religious functions—sectarianism, recognition of various kinds of differences and the custom of untouchability have given rise to mutual hatred and hostilities, and these are exercising unobstructed sway and are saturating the national life with all sorts of misery, destitution and distress. Thus it is evident that, whether in the East or in the West, the clinging to these outrageous views and this contemptible attitude towards men and nations, with the consequent monstrous behaviour they engender, is the root cause of all the malice and hostility rampant in the world. The service of man, looking upon him as Narayana, initiated by Swamiji, is the only means of solving this most difficult problem. With this end in view, Swamiji placed before the whole of mankind this highest ideal, instinct with universal equality, amity, and same-sightedness, and has charged men to regulate and model their lives in all spheres,

in religion, society and statecraft and even in the small acts of their daily lives, after that ideal. To preach this great ideal to the world and indicate the means of its fruition is the end and aim of the Ramakrishna Math and the Ramakrishna Mission founded by Swami Vivekananda.

* * *

348. God is Love and Law combined in one—all love and mercy as the Mother, and dispenser of justice as the Father. He is the giver of the fruits of action, as well as the destroyer of the fetters of fate of those who take refuge in Him.

* * *

349. The wind collects the clouds and the wind drives them away again. Clouds hide the sun, so does Maya the Self. When clouds disperse, the sun shines. Mind creates bondage, and it is the mind also which removes bondage. When Maya is destroyed within, the Self shines in Its own glory. Maya is only a passing phantom. How can it reveal the Self which is eternally real and self-manifest?

* * *

350. Swamiji has said: Sri Ramakrishna's

ideas of reconciliation of all religions and
of Universal Religion should not only
be preached to the world as a training
and an ideal, but have to be made practical and effective in daily life. That is to
say, we have to reflect in our life by our
daily actions the spirituality of the Hindus,
the compassion to all beings of the Bud-
dhists, the organised activity of the Chris-
tians and the spirit of brotherhood among
the Muslims. With this object in view, we
have to establish the Universal Religion
among all mankind irrespective of caste,
creed and colour.

*　　　*　　　*

351. Hinduism begat Buddhism, Buddhism begat Christianity, Christianity begat
Mohammedanism. All these four religions
must meet and blend together in India in
the modern age to form a harmonious
whole. To accomplish this mission Sri
Ramakrishna was born—to compose quarrels and fights of the children and grand-
children and establish peace and goodwill
on earth again. Thus says Swami Vivekananda!

352. All your life you have listened to plenty of spiritual advice and have had enough instruction to guide you. You know enough of religious precepts yourself, and surely proffer them to others also. But who is going to listen to you, unless you can show that you have practised at least a part of the teachings in your own life? There is a world of difference between profession and practice. It is not necessary for one's salvation to read and listen to a mass of scriptures and sermons. If you can put into practice in your life even so much as a single precept in regard to the path of Liberation, you will feel blessed and the world will also be benefited. And by the grace of the Mother of the Universe, you will depart this life to the realm of Bliss, crossing the shoreless ocean of existence!

* * *

353. Brothers! We came out of the mother's womb naked and alone. We have to depart from this world also alone. No one will accompany us, even our dearest ones who cannot live a moment without us, nor we without them. Neither can we take

along with us any of our cherished possessions which are dearer than our life. The
newborn's cry was the sign of its life and
was hailed with delight by others. Let
others cry at your passing, but you depart
with calm and peace, with unearthly joy
and bliss welling up in your countenance
from the unfathomed depths of your being.
Then you will have truly lived your life.
Then life will have no charm and death
no terrors for you. You will have conquered both life and death. You will find
yourself in the realm which is beyond life
and death, beyond bondage and Mukti,
beyond light and darkness, beyond good and
evil, beyond pleasure and pain—far, far away
from all the dual pairs of opposites. It is the
realm of knowing yourself, of finding yourself as you really are. It is the realm of Peace
everlasting, realm of Existence-Knowledge-
Bliss Absolute. If you aspire to reach this
eternal realm, the Goal Supreme of life,
shake off all Maya, all attachment to the
unreal, follow the teachings of the Masters,
the perfected beings, the seers of Truth,
and attune yourself with their spirit. The
Goal will be easier of attainment with the

help of such a *Sad-Guru*, the visible representative of your Chosen Ideal. This is the whole of Truth, the gist of the teachings of all scriptures—He alone is Real, all else is false! *Tat twamasi*! and Thou art That! This is the ultimate truth which must come to every man and woman in this life or after endless rounds of birth and death, according to the Law of Nature.

May you, my own dear self, realise the Truth even now by the Grace of God and be free from this moment for ever and evermore! Lord bless you all!

Om! Shantih! Shantih! Shantih! Om!

Om! Peace be to you and to me! Peace be within and without, everywhere! Peace be to all beings! Peace be on earth and in all the spheres of the Heavens!

Peace! Peace! Peace!
Om! Om! Om!

GLOSSARY

Abhih—Abhih—Be fearless! Be fearless!

Abhyâsa—Repeated and sustained efforts, particularly, to make the mind steady.

Abhyâsa-Yoga—The path of repeated or continued practice resulting in the concentration or absorption of the mind.

Achârya-Koti—An exclusive type of exalted spiritual personage born with the mission of propagating spiritual truths, being themselves perfect by nature. The World-Teacher.

Adesha—Direct Divine Command.

Adhikâravâda—The doctrine of special rights and privileges conferred by the Shastras upon those castes and classes who have the necessary qualifications according to their peculiar mental make-up or hereditary capacity to perform certain specified duties, civil, sacrificial, religious etc., or upon those deserving aspirants who desire to take up a particular course of spiritual practice. Its principles being too exclusive have been unduly exploited by the priest-craft and subjected to much abuse stunting the growth of Hindu society.

Adrishta—*Lit.* Not seen. The unseen result of good or bad actions done in some previous state of existence and experienced in another; hence, unaccounted for. Destiny.

Aham—The Ego—'I-ness'.

Ahimsa—Non-injury, non-violence.

Aparigraha—Non-acceptance of gifts.

Arâtrika—Evening service with waving of lights etc. before the Deity.

Arjuna—The great epic personality of the *Mahâbhârata* to whom Sri Krishna preached the Gita on the battlefield of Kurukshetra. See also Pândavas, *q.v.*

Âsana—A particular posture or mode of sitting for practice of concentration.

Âshramas—Stages of Life. They are four in number—Brahmacharya, *q.v.*, Gârhasthya —the stage of a householder, Vânaprastha— the stage of the recluse, and Sannyâsa, *q.v.*

Atithi—A traveller who halts in someone's house for a free meal and rest. Entertaining such a guest is considered a sacred duty of a householder.

Âtman—The Self; The Absolute; Brahman. The Witness.

Âvatâra—Incarnation of God in physical form.

Avidyâ—Primal ignorance; Nescience.

Belur Math—Monastery of the Ramakrishna Order of Monks at Belur, on the western bank of the Gangâ, four miles from Calcutta, established by Swami Vivekananda in 1898 as the headquarters of the Ramakrishna Math and the Mission.

Bhakta—A devotee; an aspirant who follows the path of devotion or love.

Bhakta Vidura—The name of this devotee is found in the *Mahâbhârata*. He is looked upon as an ideal of humility.

Bhakti-Yoga—The path of union with the Lord through intense love or devotion.

Bhâva—The blessed mood of spiritual ecstasy. Emotion expressing a particular relationship with God in which one is absorbed.

Bhâva-mukha—That spiritual state which one experiences as being on the borderline between the Relative and the Supersensuous, to both of which he has access at will. It comes to one who is born with a Divine Mission, who coming down from the highest state engages himself in doing good to the world.

Bhikshuni—A Buddhist nun.

Bhoga—Enjoyment of worldly objects.

Bibhuti—Occult and superhuman powers.

Brahmachârin—An initiate who has taken the vow of continence.

Brahmacharya—Vow of perfect continence; Restraint of the senses and sexual indulgence, which means renunciation of lustful desire, that is, chastity in thought, word and deed. Celibate students' life of purity.

Brahman—The One Existence, the Absolute.

Chaitanya—One of the outstanding spiritual personalities of Bengal regarded as an Incarnation of God. He preached the path of Devotion.

Chakras—Nerve centres in the spinal column.

Chandâla—A member of the lowest strata of society. An untouchable.

Châpâti—Unleavened bread baked over an open fire.

Châtak—A species of small bird. Its peculiar character is believed to be not to drink other than rain-water.

Chhâtu—Barley fried and powdered fine.

Dâdâ—Elder brother. A Bengali word.

Dama—Restraint of the external senses.

Devas—The shining ones, semi-divine states attained by works of good desire.

Dharma—Religion; Righteousness; Moral Law; A prescribed course of conduct in relation to a particular stage of life.

Dhyâna—Meditation.

Draupadi—The wife of the five Pandava brothers—Yudhisthira, Bhima, Arjuna, Nakula and Sahadeva.

Gangâ—the Holy river of the Hindus. Ganga-water is considered sacred; used for purification and Puja, q.v.

Ghantâ-nârâr-dal—*Lit*. those who only ring the bell in doing worship. A contemptuous term for those who look upon the ceremonial part of religion as its whole and actually do nothing to build the spiritual life. This term is coined by Swami Vivekananda himself.

Gomukhi—The source of the Gangâ in the snowy regions of the Himalayas.

Gunas—Aspects of the Cosmic Energy—Sattva, Rajas, and Tamas, q.v.

Guru—Spiritual Guide; The Preceptor from whom Mantra-Dikshâ is received.

Guru-Dakshinâ—The humble and respectful offering to the Guru by the disciple at the time of Initiation.

Guru-Paramparâ—The traditional line of the Gurus. A mystic spiritual power flows along the line of such Gurus which cannot be had without their help.

Haridâs—A Muslim disciple of Chaitanya.

Harishchandra—One of the prominent epic characters that are perennial sources of inspiration to the Hindus. King Harishchandra became immortal by his bravely suffering untold miseries for his adherence to Truth.

Hitopadesha—A primary Sanskrit book of short stories imparting very instructive moral lessons.

Ishta—Chosen Ideal or Deity.

Ishwara-Koti—An exclusive type of exalted spiritual personage born with Divine Knowledge and Authority for the spiritual uplift of the people.

Japa—Continual repetition of the Mantra, *q.v.*

Jiva—Individual self.

Jnâna—Knowledge of the Eternal Truth.

Jnâna-Yoga—The path of Knowledge.

Jnâna-Yogi—Jnânin, Jnâni—One who follows the Path of Knowledge, particularly, knowledge of the Divinity, or the Supreme Self.

Kâli (Shyâmâ)—Dark-hued; name of God as Divine Mother in Her benign-terrible form dancing on the prostrate body of Shiva. It has a deep mystical meaning.

Kalpa—A periodic cycle of creation and dissolution of the Universe. A period of 432,000,000 years measuring the duration of the world.

Kamsa—A tyrant king of Mathurâ, who was Sri Krishna's maternal uncle. He imprisoned his pregnant sister being warned by an etherial voice to kill the new-born babe, Krishna, as he was destined to destroy him.

But his scheme was thwarted by Divine Dispensation and he was later killed by grown-up Krishna.

Karma—Action; Work; Duty; Ritualistic work; Result of past actions. The Law of cause and effect in the moral world.

Karma-Yoga—The path of selfless work done unattached to the result thereof.

King Duryodhana—The wicked leader of the hundred sons of Dhritarâshtra, who conspired the exile of the Pandavas, deprived them of their kingdom, waged war and was finally conquered by the latter and met death with all his brothers and allies at Kurukshetra. The story is depicted in the epic, the *Mahabharata*.

Kumbhaka—Retention of breath. A process of Râja-Yoga.

Kundalini—The coiled-up; the sleeping Divine power in all beings.

Lâlâ Babu—A big landlord of an aristocratic family of Calcutta who renounced the world immediately on hearing a suggestive word to burn all desires into ashes on the fast approach of the ebbing out of life.

Lilâ—Divine sport; Creation looked upon as a Divine Play.

Mâdhukari-bhikshâ—Collecting morsels of cooked food from a number of houses, as a bee gathers honey from different flowers. Food obtained by begging thus is considered pure.

Mahâbhâva—The superb ecstatic state of God-intoxication experienced by Avatâras.

Mahâmâyâ—The great Conjuror of Cosmic

Illusion. The Divine Mother who has also become the Cosmic Illusion, is so called.

Mahâ Purusha—A great soul; Saint; Seer.

Mahâvira (Hanumâna)—Ideal Brahmacharin and servant of the Lord—the embodiment of faith and service; the Great lieutenant of Rama during his war against Râvana, *q.v.* Possessed of supreme devotion for Rama whom he knew to be the very Incarnation of God, he attained the Knowledge of Self.

Mantra—A sacred word; or a mystic symbol of the Chosen Ideal or Deíty, imparted by the Guru, through which the initiated meditates on God in a particular Divine Form or Idea.

Mantra-Dikshâ—Dikshâ; Initiation of the aspirant by the Guru into the process of spiritual practice, introducing him to a mystic name or word-symbol of God.

Master—Sri Ramakrishna.

Mâyâ—Ignorance. Illusion. The mysterious Power through which the illusory cosmos is projected by God.

Medhâ—Retentive faculty and intuition.

Moksha, Mukti—Liberation from all bondage —freedom from birth and death.

Mumukshu—One desiring and endeavouring to attain Mukti, *q.v.* or Salvation.

Naivedya—Offering of washed rice, fruits and sweets, or sugar only to a Deity.

Nara-Nârâyana—Nara=Man. Divinity in humanity. Hence *Nara-Nârâyana Sevâ* means to serve man seeing God in him.

Nârâyana—An epithet of Vishnu as the controller of the Universe.

Nirvâna—Annihilation of the Cosmic Illusion. Complete extinction of individual or worldly existence.

Nirvikalpa-Samâdhi—Superconscious state of experiencing absolute oneness with the Universal Spirit.

Nishkâma Karma—Work without any desire for fruits; selfless work.

Pându—A king of the Lunar Race. Father of the five Pandavas. See Draupadi, q.v.

Paramahamsa—One who has perfectly renounced the world, and is devoid of the feeling of identification with the body. The highest stage of a Sannyasin, q.v.

Parigraha—Acceptance of gifts.

Patanjali—One of the authors of the six different schools of thought about the knowledge of God found in the Vedas. His system of philosophy (Darshana) is known as Yoga. The treatise is called the *Pâtanjala Yoga Sutras* (Aphorisms).

Prahlâda—Son of Hiranyakashipu, the king of the demons. He was a selfless devotee of God—Vishnu. His father subjected him to all sorts of cruelties to get rid of him, but Prahlada came out unscathed. Hiranyakashipu in a fit of exasperation challenged him to prove the omnipresence of his Vishnu in the pillar before him and kicked it, and out came Vishnu, half-man and half-lion and tore him to pieces.

Prakriti—Nature; Original source of the material world; Causal State; Cosmic Energy.

Pralaya—The dissolution of the whole universe at the end of each cycle.

Prâna—The vital Forces in the body. The sum-total of the Cosmic Energy.

Prânâyâma—Controlling the Prana; breathing exercise to concentrate the mind.

Prema—Love; Supreme devotion for God.

Pujâ—Worship.

Punya—Work of religious merit; Virtue.

Purânas—Eighteen sacred works of ancient or legendary history containing the whole body of Hindu mythology.

Purusha—The Pure Spirit; The Soul.

Purushakàra—Self-effort; manliness.

Râgânugâ-Bhakti—Supreme devotion which comes after the purest and deepest attachment to God as one's Beloved.

Râjasika—Energetic, ambitious, passionate and restless qualities in man due to the predominance of Rajas—the dynamic aspect of Cosmic Energy.

Râja-Yoga—The science of conquering the internal nature, for the purpose of freeing the Purusha, that is, realising the Divinity in every being.

Râma—An Incarnation of God.

Râmaprasâda—The celebrated Bengali devotee and saint. His devotional songs to his Divine Mother Kâli are a source of perennial inspiration.

Rasagolla—Juicy, spongy Bengali sweet. The round balls which float in syrup are a product of specially turned milk.

Râvana—King of Lankâ, the demon who abducted Sita, the wife of Sri Ramachandra —an Incarnation of God. The story is depicted in the epic, the *Ramayana*.

21

Rishi—Seer of Truth; A sage.

Sad-Guru—A spiritual teacher who is knower of Brahman, who has realised Truth.

Sâdhaka—Aspirant practising Sâdhanâ or spiritual discipline for realising God.

Sâdhu—Monk, a holy man.

Samâdhâna—Fixing the mind in abstract contemplation on the true nature of the Spirit.

Samâdhi—Superconsciousness; Profound concentration attained by spiritual practices.

Samsâra—The world; the course of worldly life; transmigratory existence.

Samskâras—Impressions in the mind-stuff that produce habits and tendencies; resultant tendencies of the past thoughts and deeds.

Samyama—Restraint of mind and the senses.

Sannyâsin—Monk; one who has completely renounced the world, belonging to the last stage of Hindu life.

Sattra, Chhattra—Feeding-house for mendicants, maintained by the charity of wealthy householders, mostly of the trading community, who desire to earn *Punya* for themselves and their ancestors.

Sattva—The principle of goodness or purity.

Sâttvica—Having the Sattva quality developed, endowed with purity, equanimity, and clear vision.

Satya—Truth.

Savikalpa-Samâdhi—The ecstatic state of consciousness in which the devotee is absorbed in the blissful relationship with his Chosen Deity either as a child, mother, friend, or the Beloved, etc.

Sevâ—Service. Consecrated work.

Sevya-Sevaka—Sevya means one who is served, and Sevaka means one who serves. Sevya-Sevaka refers to the deep and loving relationship between the one who is served and the one who serves.

Shakti—Divine Energy; the dynamic aspect of the Eternal Being as creating, preserving and destroying the universe, called as the Divine Mother.

Shama—Absence or restraint of passions. Tranquillity of mind.

Shâstras—The Hindu Scriptures.

Shishupâla—A king who was a sworn enemy of Krishna. He denounced him before the august gathering of King Yudhisthira's Râjasuya Yajna or Sacrifice for commemorating over-all sovereignty. His head was cut off by Krishna with his Disc.

Shraddhâ—Dynamic and unflinching faith in the words of the Guru and the Scriptures.

Shrâddha—Sacramental ceremonies performed for the welfare of the departed.

Siddha—One who has reached the Goal, particularly, attained spiritual Illumination. A perfected being or a Yogi who has gained supernatural powers.

Siddha-Mantra—Mystic name-symbol of the Chosen Ideal or Deity, which is capable of leading to the attainment of God.

Siddhis—Occult and superhuman powers attained by the practice of Yoga.

Sthitadhi—Person of steady wisdom free from all attachment, hence a knower of Brahman.

Swâdhyâya—Study of the Scriptures.

Tamas—Darkness, Inertia, Ignorance; the lowest aspect of Cosmic Energy. It veils the Reality.

Tâmasika—Individual in whom Tamas, producing inertia and ignorance, is predominant. Also, such a nature or character.

Tâmbula—Betel-leaf of a creeper chewed by Indians, prepared with lime, catechu, arecanut and spices.

Tantra—A series of sacred works presenting God as Divine Mother and prescribing elaborate esoteric rituals.

Tântrika—Follower of Tantra.

Tapasyâ—The practice of austerity.

Tapovana—Hermitage. The forest-dwelling of an anchorite who lives in seclusion to pursue his spiritual life undisturbed.

Târâ—A particular terrible form or aspect of the Divine Mother.

Titikshâ—Maintaining the calm of mind and remaining unaffected or resigned amidst all kinds of afflictions and provocations.

Tolâ—Indian measure, one tolâ is equivalent to 2/5th oz.

Udbodhan—The Bengali monthly organ of Ramakrishna Math and Mission, published from Calcutta. It was started by Swami Vivekananda.

Uparati—Abstaining from sexual enjoyment, resulting in calm of mind.

Upâsanâ—Lit. sitting near. Worship or meditation of God or Deity. Religious service or prayer.

Vairâgya—Dispassion; Aversion to enjoyment of sense-objects in this life or in the next.

Vaishnavas—Hindu sect worshipping God as Vishnu, *q.v.* Krishna etc.

Vedas—The oldest scripture of the world. All other Hindu scriptures owe their origin and inspiration to the Vedas. The Vedas are supposed to have been directly revealed by the Supreme Being, Brahman, and their authority is not questioned by any of the six systems of Hindu philosophy. From root Vid=to know.

Vidyâ—Knowledge. Science.

Vilvamangal—A legendary personality who attained Blessedness by spiritual austerities when his all-consuming attachment to a public woman was turned towards God by her sharp reproof.

Vishnu—The Chosen Deity of the Vaishnavas. One of the Hindu Trinity—God as Preserver.

Viveka—Discrimination between the Truth and the un-truth, the Real and the un-real.

Yama—The God of death. Internal purification through self-control.

Yoga—Joining; Joining the lower with the higher self. Union with God.

Yogi—Aspirant practising special course of Yoga discipline to attain union with God.

Yuga-Dharma—The religion of the age; the prevailing religious idea of the time.

APPRECIATIONS

I

Here is a small book by Swami Virajananda, the present head of the Ramakrishna Math and Mission, which sheds white radiance on the path to spiritual awareness, so vividly described by the ancient Indian sages as "dark with distance and sharp as the razor's edge". This modern Indian sage also makes it abundantly clear that the path is no easy one to tread, but for those with courage to set their stumbling feet upon the way, Swami Virajananda offers much helpful advice. Indian aspirants will find his teachings quite in harmony with accepted Indian methods. Westerners are likely to find them more difficult to put into practice, partly because the pattern of thought is less familiar in Protestant countries, partly because the inescapable and ceaseless activity of modern Western life seriously interferes with the individual's right to privacy, an essential for the meditative practices here recommended.

Yet it is in the West above all that a reorientation of thought and a reappraisal of values have become long overdue. Is there not something vitally wrong in the mode of living out of which have come two tragic global wars within three decades of the twentieth century, and which permits even today the glib talk of a World War III? For too many people, civilization has become confused with multiplicity of material possessions and the fever-chart of an ever-rising standard of comfort. If human life has no higher achievement to strive for, is it really worth while? India answers boldly that there is a higher purpose, namely, spiritual awareness and knowledge of the Divine, based on actual direct perception or experience. Such knowledge alone can give us the true standard by which to judge ourselves in the context, not of what we have, but what we are or are sincerely trying to become.

In an age of technology and specialization, it should at once be grasped that spiritual progress is not possible without practice, yet it is assumed that mere mental curiosity or intellectual affirmation, the reading of a few books or perhaps the prescribed number of visits to a psychoanalyst, is all that is required to clear away the jungles obstructing the vision of Divine Reality. How different the Indian exaction from the individual of utmost strenuous resolve and strenuous effort, as taught in these earnest pages! But Swami Virajananda assures us—and why should we doubt his words?—that control of body and mind will gradually transform the clay vessel into a worthy receptacle for Truth.

—GERTRUDE EMERSON SEN *

II

I had the great privilege to re-type the manuscript of Swami Virajananda's "Paramartha Prasanga" which is going to be published in the U.S. Typing the script was just like studying it thoroughly and I benefited a great

---

* Gertrude Emerson Sen is the author of "The Pageants of India's History".

deal from it. . . . He must be a treasure-house of information and spirituality. . . . Maha-maya's delusive power is very great and as Swami Virajananda points out so lucidly in his book, "the immediacy of the pleasure derived from the enjoyment of sense objects is the un-doing of man. Even a grain of noumenal pleas-ure makes one forget the pains of miseries suffered a million times". That is describing Mother's power in the shortest way. It is like putting it in a nutshell. In another place Swami Virajananda says: "As is the mental concep-tion, so is the attainment. We get what we seek—no less, no more!" This again proves the importance of a greatly developed power of imagination.

—HILARY HOLT *

III

. . . I agree with the two Introductions, which are nicely put, that "Paramartha Pra-sanga" will appeal to seekers of Truth because of its directness and sincerity. Who knows— it may become one of those books that conti-nues to be printed from age to age, like Brother Lawrence's "Practice of the Presence of God", which also has that simple, direct quality.

—AN AMERICAN DEVOTEE

* Hilary Holt is a noted Austro-American writer and author of several books of short stories.